Talcott Williams

The Story of a Woman's Municipal Campaign by the Civic Club for School Reform of Philadelphia

Talcott Williams

**The Story of a Woman's Municipal Campaign by the Civic Club for School Reform
of Philadelphia**

ISBN/EAN: 9783337296421

Printed in Europe, USA, Canada, Australia, Japan

Cover: Foto ©Thomas Meinert / pixelio.de

More available books at **www.hansebooks.com**

PUBLICATIONS OF
THE AMERICAN ACADEMY OF POLITICAL AND SOCIAL SCIENCE.
NO. 150.

The Story

OF A

Woman's Municipal Campaign

By the Civic Club

FOR

SCHOOL REFORM

In the Seventh Ward of

PHILADELPHIA.

EDITED BY

MRS. TALCOTT WILLIAMS.

PHILADELPHIA:
AMERICAN ACADEMY OF POLITICAL AND SOCIAL SCIENCE.
1895.

NOTE.

The early stages of each new form of political activity are always difficult of study, and every student has found this as true of the reform movement of yesterday, as of the beginnings of a national constitution a century old. The growing political activity of women is developing both in aim, canvass and organization, and women who come fresh to political work see some of the evils of politics with a clearer vision than those inured by use to abuse. In the Philadelphia municipal election of February, 1895, the Civic Club, a reform organization of women, began its work for school reform by endeavoring to secure the election of women as Ward School Directors. In the Seventh Ward, an active campaign and canvass were made by women for two women candidates, Mrs. Sophia Wells Royce Williams and Mrs. Eliza Butler Kirkbride. The following pages contain the reports laid before the Civic Club on this canvass, and submitted by it to the American Academy of Political and Social Science. They describe the personal experiences of the candidates, the method, means and personnel of organization, the character and conditions of ward political life, its vote and political organizations, the cause of failure and the path to ultimate success. These minute reports of a local ward struggle over a school office are printed as a permanent contribution to the political history of the day, because the record of one such contest throws light on all.

331 South 16th St.   TALCOTT WILLIAMS.

PREFACE.

The attention of students of the body politic on either its political or social side is centred for the most part on its wider areas and its broader issues. The town, from its historical importance and its current hopeful political activity, has received its full share of attention. The city ward has had little. It would be difficult to cite a study of political activity in this primary civic unit, giving its conditions, the helps and hindrances to healthy political action, the political organizations which control it, and the difficulties in the way of their reform.

Yet, exactly as effective political improvement in the country at large must begin in the town, and the political health of the State is only possible, as the town enjoys a healthy political freedom and activity, so civic reform is only possible when the ward has been attacked, carried and reformed. If those who seek political progress and reform cannot influence for better things the ward in which they live and are known, how can they hope to influence the city in which they are less known? Reform movements are constantly left in the air, polling a vote ridiculously small by comparison with the noise they have made, because they have not begun with the ward and matured a ward organization before attacking the city. Thanks to careful organization in the present canvass, the expected vote was doubled.

The Civic Club of Philadelphia, was organized January 1, 1894, and has a membership of five hundred. It has for its object, " To promote by education and active co-operation a higher public spirit and a better social order."

It has had, from its organization, the same president, and as secretary, Miss Cornelia Frothingham. It is divided

(3)

for purposes of action and organization into four departments: Municipal, Educational, Social Science, and Art, of
which Mrs. N. Dubois Miller, Miss Anna Hallowell, Mrs.
William F. Jenks and Mrs. C. Stuart Patterson, were respectively chairmen in the winter of 1894–95. In the course
of its general efforts to improve the schools of Philadelphia,
two of its members were nominated by the regular Municipal
League and Democratic organizations for school directors in
the Seventh Ward. Such nominations are usually accepted
passively by the women who receive them, and who share
the fate and fortune of the ticket of which they are a part.
In the present instance, it was determined to make an independent canvass for the election of these two women, without
any hope of success, but as a public duty, and a step in the
political education of the members of the club. In the course
of this canvass, a ward organization by election districts was
made, one of the most complete, if not the most complete,
ever effected in Philadelphia by a reform movement, the election district being habitually neglected by reformers. For
three weeks this organization made an active house to house
canvass. In all, 13,000 visits were paid, thirty-seven meetings were held, $422.80 were expended, and 146 women were
enlisted in the active work of the campaign.

This canvass met all the difficulties and ended in the failure common to such reform movements; but it is by failure
like this that the seeds of success are sown. In the right
cause, no such thing as failure exists. In the end, in the last
high sense, every effort in its behalf is success.

Throughout this brief, but vigorous, campaign records
were kept, names registered and reports planned, in order to
preserve for future use and guidance the experience of this
effort and organization. At its close, a series of reports were
prepared, giving all its phases. They are printed in the
present form as "original documents" which present to the
student of political and social action, as nothing else can,
the work and working of a reform ward canvass. The field

is narrow, the contest humble, the office relative to the world's larger prizes insignificant, but it is in fields like this, in contests of this character, by the reform of our ward schools, that freedom's battle must to-day be fought and won or lost through the supine indifference of the refined, the educated and the well-to-do.

SARA Y. STEVENSON,
237 South 21st St.   *President.*

TABLE OF CONTENTS.

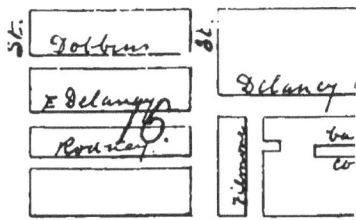

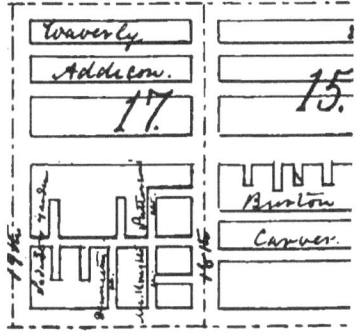

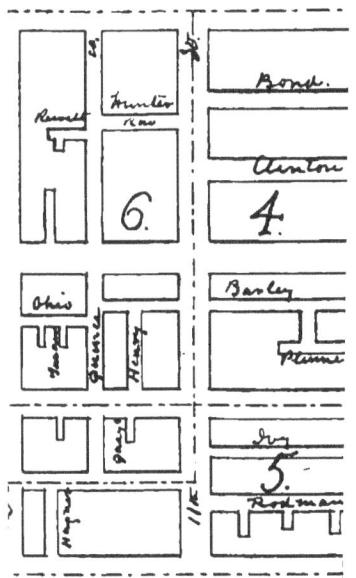

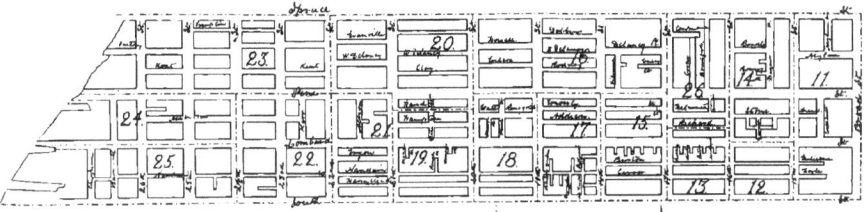
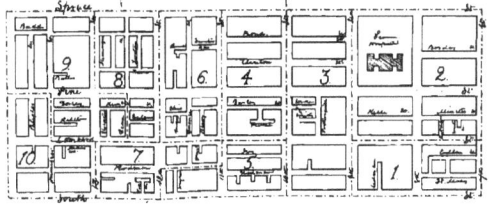

SEVENTH
WARD.

INTRODUCTION.

The present school system of Philadelphia is a piece of patchwork left over from ancient days—and in its fitness for creating disorder might almost be called a crazy quilt. It comes down to us from the time when the city was an aggregation of villages, each having its local interests intact, and its schools organized under its own special school board. These were united under a central body called the Board of Control consisting of one delegate from each local organization.

While the villages had distinctive character, and local interests and local pride, the local boards fairly represented the citizens of the neighborhood; but as the city wiped out the dividing lines, and party politics gained control, and the school board became the field of operation for party workers, the degeneration in it began, and has continued steadily until the present time.

At first the Central Board was appointed by the local boards and shared in their deterioration, but through the efforts of Mr. Edward Shippen and others, the appointing power was in 1867 transferred to the judges of the courts, where it now resides.

Women have been eligible to all the school boards of Pennsylvania since the adoption of the new constitution in 1874. There are now, in the State at large, about forty women serving as school directors. Immediately on the passage of the act, a couple of women were elected to the school board of the Thirteenth Section in this city. They met with much opposition, however, and on the expiration of their terms were not re-nominated, and for several years the experiment was not repeated. Finally, in the spasm of reform which passed over the city in 1881–83, some members of the Committee of One Hundred turned their attention to the improvement of the ward school boards, and secured the nomination of two women in the Twenty-ninth Section. These women stood for the office, on principle, because they believed women should share in the control of their children's education. They had no idea the movement would prove popular, and were most astonished when they found they had not only been elected, but had run ahead of the regular ticket. The work of the women seemed to commend itself to the voters of that locality, for two women have served continuously on that board for a period of fourteen years. The politicians once attempted to leave Dr. Rachel Bodley off the ticket, but the people set up an independent movement and returned her again in triumph. A woman has at times served to fill unexpired terms on the Board of the Twenty-fourth Ward. With these exceptions the four hundred and fifty-two school directors in the thirty-seven districts or wards of the city, are men.

The school system of Philadelphia needs re-organization through and through. Most of the large cities of the United States are now wrestling with this problem. New York and Brooklyn had bills to this end before the Legislature at Albany. Boston made a distinct educational advance in putting her school administration more decidedly into the hands of experts. Education is a science. Every chance citizen cannot administer it.

If Philadelphia can accomplish re-organization through legislative action, it is the thing most of all to be desired. But if the local boards are to remain for some little time longer, it is our manifest duty to place upon them women of fine intelligence and earnestness, such as we have recently offered to the Seventh Ward. It is the only remedial agency, through which we can hope to put life into the old sectional board system, now tottering to its grave, having outlived its usefulness and the love of the people who created it.

1401 North 17th St.   MARY E. MUMFORD.

WOMEN ON LOCAL SCHOOL BOARDS.

The revised Constitution of Pennsylvania, adopted by the vote of the people, December 16, 1873, and proclaimed by Governor John F. Hartranft, January 7, 1874, in Article X, Section 3, reads, "Women twenty-one years of age and upwards shall be eligible to any office of control or management under the school laws of this State."

Since the adoption of this clause in our constitution, five wards of the city of Philadelphia have claimed the privilege of having women on their local school boards.

To Mrs. Harriet W. Paist and Mrs. Letitia P. Woelpper, of the Thirteenth Ward, we owe a debt of gratitude for being the first women to allow their names to be placed on an electoral ticket. Upon Mrs. Paist fell the pioneer and difficult work of securing the election, for such it was, although the right was clearly defined in the new code of laws of our State.

The aphorism, "History repeats itself," was most forcibly demonstrated in this local campaign of 1874. Mrs. Paist did not seek the office of school director. She was called upon by members of the Republican Executive Committee of the Thirteenth Ward and asked if she would accept the nomination. I have not discovered what prompted or inspired them to commit this radical and unprecedented act, perhaps, however, a temporary hallucination, as facts later may induce us to believe. Mrs. Paist accepted the offer in all good faith. It did not take long, however, for the hallucination to pass, for as if awakening from a dream, the committee, realizing what they had done, began at once to try and untie the knot which they had made. It was no use; the harder they tried, the tighter it became. We are appalled at the means to which they resorted ! First, under the guise of friendship, each candidate was visited separately. Mrs. Woelpper was told that Mrs. Paist had resigned, and that it would not be pleasant for her, Mrs. Woelpper, to serve on the board alone. Mrs. Paist was told the same concerning Mrs. Woelpper. The next effort was one of policy. Fearing that the election of a councilman would be jeopardized if the names of the women were not withdrawn, the committee persistently urged their retiring, but without success, concerning which action Mrs. Paist forcibly remarked, "I did not know before, that we women held the balance of power." Finally, at a meeting of the Republican Executive Committee a forged letter was read, purporting to come from Mrs. Paist, offering her resignation. Through the watchfulness and protection of Mr. F. Theodore Walton, a member of the committee, who faithfully stood by the candidate during this trying period, Mrs. Paist was informed of what was to take place and was ready with a reply, which was read by Mr. Walton at the meeting, immediately after the reading of the forged letter, declaring the latter to be a forgery, and that she had no intention of resigning.

Here was a refined and honest woman, asked, in good faith, to take an office of trust and honor in our city government, heaped with abuse and dishonor by those who should have been proud to be her associates in the work of education.

There are always two sides, the serious and the humorous —she was the victim of forgery, accused of being a Quaker, of beating her husband, and of spelling chairman without an i, surely she must show herself to the public in order to vindicate her true character. Encouraged and strengthened by her husband and by her firm friend Mr. Walton, a mass meeting was held in her behalf in Mænnerchor Hall, Fairmount Avenue. This was in every sense a mass meeting, for the house was packed from pit to dome and at the entrance of the candidate the band burst forth with "Hail to the

Chief!'' Mr. Walton presided and the audience listened
to the following concise address made by Mrs. Paist:

Mr. President, Ladies and Gentlemen—'' ' Hear me for my
cause and be silent that you may hear: believe me for mine
honor and have respect unto mine honor that you may
believe.'

''I appear before you this evening as one of the regular
Republican candidates for school director and hold in my
hand a certificate of election signed by Charles M. Carpenter,
president; James M. Stewart and David T. Smith, clerks.
If after this right guaranteed to us under the new constitution it is to be thus wrested from us by a few designing politicians who have luxuriated at the public crib, I ask you
where is all our boasted freedom, freedom of thought and
action?

'' I have been taught to believe that after being regularly
nominated and receiving the majority of votes at the primary
election, the matter was fixed until it came before the people
for their decision at the regular election.   This meeting
has not been called in the interest of politics but to defend
the cause of justice, truth and right and expose the corruption that now exists in the Republican party, the party I
have been so proud to call my own, although Alderman
Carpenter was pleased to say I had no party because I was
not a voter; this you will perceive is good, sound logic, coming
as it did from such a very worthy exponent of the law, but
in the language of United States Senator Carpenter this is
in the immediate future, and this course of proceeding will
only hasten the day.   Desperate are these politicians in their
death throes, for doomed they are to political death and
destruction.   ' Those whom the gods would destroy they
first make mad.'   Having emancipated ourselves so recently
from the thralldom of African slavery, shall we now bow our
heads and tamely submit to this political yoke being welded
around our necks, or shall we rise in our might and shake
it off?

" Peter Lane, Jr., not satisfied with being one of the main actors in the plot to defeat my election that has been so fully exposed through the public prints, has resorted to slurring my name.   ' Who steals my purse, steals trash ; 'tis something, nothing : 'twas mine, 'tis his, and has been slave to thousands ; but he that filches from me my good name, robs me of that which not enriches him and makes me poor indeed.'   What have I done to merit such treatment?   I have neither forged a letter, been guilty of bribery nor placing in my pocket moneys that should have gone into the city or State treasury.

"And now, in conclusion, I leave it with the voters of the Thirteenth Ward to say if this outrage shall go unrebuked at the polls on February 17, 1874.''

On February 17, 1874, a large vote was polled which elected the women candidates.   The death of Mrs. Woelpper, who was a great invalid during the campaign, occurred before the expiration of the year.   Her place was filled by Mr. Thomas Steel, who died within a month.   Mrs. Paist then endeavored to have the vacancy filled by the election of Mrs. Emilie B. Coates, but was defeated, Mrs. Paist having the support of only one of her associates, that of Mr. John C. Yeager.

Her experience while serving on the board was varied. The first two years of her term were unpleasant and trying. She was evidently in a place where she was not wanted, and a disposition to crowd her out was very apparent.   Tradesmen tried to make it an object to her to use her influence in their favor, and one father offered her one hundred dollars if she would vote for his daughter as teacher.   When she mentioned this, later, in a meeting, much indignation was expressed, and the remark made, that such a thing was never heard of until a woman came upon the board.   "Certainly not,'' was Mrs. Paist's reply, "if I had taken the bribe I should not have reported it ! ''   Her last year was more agreeable in every way ; old members went out, and new ones were elected, who, if they were not in sympathy with the intruder, were certainly more courteous.

At the close of the term of three years, Mrs. Paist was renominated, but failed to secure the election.

To give a detailed account of the experiences of the remaining eight women who have been elected to serve on local boards would take too much space. I will, therefore, merely add their names, including those of Mrs. Paist and Mrs. Woelpper, with their respective wards:

Mrs. Harriet W. Paist,* Thirteenth Ward, 1874, 1875, 1876.

Mrs. Letitia P. Woelpper,† Thirteenth Ward, part of 1874.

Dr. Rachel L. Bodley,‡ Twenty-ninth Ward, 1882, 1883, 1884, 1887, part of 1888.

Mrs. Mary E. Mumford,§ Twenty-ninth Ward, 1882, 1883, 1884, 1885, 1886, 1887, 1888, part of 1889.

Miss Emily Sartain,‖ Twenty-ninth Ward (August 3) 1888, 1889, 1890, 1891, 1892, until September.

Dr. Annie B. Hall, Twenty-ninth Ward (September 30) 1892, 1893, 1894, 1895.

Mrs. Lucretia M. B. Mitchell, Twenty-fourth Ward, 1883, 1884, 1885.

Miss H. Kate Murdock, Twenty-fourth Ward, 1883, 1884, 1885, 1886, 1887, 1888, 1889, 1890, 1891, 1892, until March, 1893.

Mrs. Sophia Wells Royce Williams,** Eighth Ward, 1891, 1892.

Miss Anna Longstreth, Fifteenth Ward, 1895.

908 Clinton St.   EMILY HALLOWELL.

* Previous to June, 1891, members of the local school board were elected in February, but their term of service did not commence until the following January. By Act of Assembly in June, 1891, members elected to local school boards in February take their seats in April of the same year.

† Mrs. Woelpper died in a few months.

‡ Dr. Bodley died in 1888.

§ Mrs. Mumford was appointed on Board of Education in 1889.

‖ Miss Sartain resigned September, 1892.

** Mrs. Williams removed from the ward, March, 1892.

REPORT TO THE CIVIC CLUB ON WORK OF CAMPAIGN ORGANIZATION IN THE SEVENTH WARD OF PHILADELPHIA.

From January 4, to February 19, 1895.

The Committee for "Placing Women on School Boards," of the Department of Education of the Civic Club, determined, on January 4, to send to the two political parties and to the Municipal League, the names of the sixteen women residing in ten wards, who had expressed themselves as willing to serve on the school boards, if elected.

In accordance with this determination, the President of the Civic Club addressed the following circular to the Republican and Democratic leaders, as well as to the secretaries of the Municipal League in these ten wards, and to two prominent men in each of these ten wards, publishing it simultaneously in the leading newspapers of the city :

WOMEN FOR SCHOOL DIRECTORS.

It is the conviction of the Civic Club of Philadelphia, that the interests of children in our public schools would be subserved if a larger number of capable women were placed upon the Sectional School Boards. We therefore petition your body to place such women in nomination upon the regular school ticket ; and for your own convenience append the names of some women of undoubted ability who have kindly consented to serve if elected by the people :

The names are as follows :

Fifth Ward—Miss ETHEL CUSHING.

Seventh Ward—Mrs. WILLIAM P. SMITH, Mrs. WILLIAM F. JENKS, Mrs. TALCOTT WILLIAMS, Mrs. THOMAS KIRKBRIDE, Miss E. L. LOWRY and Miss E. JOSEPHINE BRAZIER.

Fourteenth Ward—Mrs. JAMES H. WINDRIM.

Fifteenth Ward—Miss ANNA LONGSTRETH.

Twentieth Ward—Mrs. S. G. MACFARLAND.

Twenty-second Ward—Mrs. MARTHA B. EARLE and Mrs. PASCHAL COGGINS.

Twenty-fourth Ward—Mrs. CHARLOTTE L. PIERCE.

Twenty-fifth Ward—Miss EDITH WETHERILL.

(14)

Twenty-seventh Ward—Mrs. JOHN SCRIBNER.

Twenty-ninth Ward—Dr. FRANCES EMILY WHITE and Mrs. J. G. LEIPER.

The only ward in which the regular Republican organization acted on this address was the Fifteenth, in which Miss Anna Longstreth was nominated, receiving on election day 6014 votes, the next highest vote for school director on the Republican ticket being 5767.

The only wards in which the Municipal League acted on this address were the Seventh, in which they nominated Mrs. Sophia W. R. Williams and Mrs. Eliza B. Kirkbride. Twenty-fourth Ward—Mrs. Charlotte L. Pierce; Twenty-ninth Ward—Mrs. J. G. Leiper—none of whom were elected.

In the following wards women were nominated for school directors by the Prohibition party, but none were elected:

Eighth Ward—ADA F. MORGAN.

Tenth Ward—CATHARINE N. CLEGG.

Fourteenth Ward—HELEN B. BIRD.

Eighteenth Ward—MARY WEST, AMANDA RAMBO ABELL.

Nineteenth Ward—AMY M. P. MOORE.

Twentieth Ward—SUSAN B. McFARLAND.

Twenty-fourth Ward—ELLA B. LUTTON.

Twenty-seventh Ward—MARY J. WILSON.

Twenty-eighth Ward—FLORENCE L. CONRAD, ANNA K. WAY.

Thirtieth Ward—MARY J. THORNTON, ADDIE H. JOHNSON.

Thirty-second Ward—A. ELIZABETH THOMAS, HANNAH H. HATTON and CAROLINE M. DODSON.

Early in January a meeting of the Municipal League of the Seventh Ward was called by the secretary, under the rules, open to every one who believed in the principle of separating city from State politics. This meeting was held at O'Neill's Hall and elected a Ward Committee of ten members at large, to which were to be added, under the rules of the Municipal League, one delegate from each of the five divisions then organized.

This committee of fifteen, nominated a ticket for councilmen and school directors, after which a ratification meeting

was held at O'Neill's Hall.   Later, pursuant to the Election
Act, nomination papers were filed with the County Commissioners, signed by not less than two per cent of the vote
cast for the candidate who received the largest vote for the
same office at the last preceding election.
The school directors' ticket was as follows :

EDWIN JAQUETT SELLERS,
Mrs. SOPHIA W. R. WILLIAMS,
Mrs. ELIZA B. KIRKBRIDE.

For future ward nominations, the Municipal League of the
Seventh Ward will only be required to file a certificate of
nomination at the County Commissioners' office, signed by
the chairman and secretary.

The Democratic ward nominating conventions met in all
of the wards, on the evening of January 15.   The convention in the Seventh Ward endorsed the three Municipal
League candidates for school directors.   The Republican
ward convention, when it met, renominated Dr. E. Clarence
Howard and Mr. S. K. Shedaker, already members of the
school board; and nominated Mr. Louis K. Esrey.

A circular was sent out by the chairman and secretary of
the Joint Committee of the Educational and Municipal Departments of the Civic Club, calling together, on January 29,
a joint meeting of these two departments, with a view to
determine three questions:

(1) Whether the members of the Civic Club in the Seventh
Ward, and other women who could be associated with them,
were willing to undertake the arduous work of a personal
canvass of the ward.

(2) If they were willing to undertake such a canvass,
would it have any effect on the voters?

(3) Would such a canvass arouse in the ward as a whole,
both men and women, a sense of responsibility for better
schools which would bear fruit in the future?

While the two candidates of the Civic Club were nominated by a reform organization and endorsed by a political

organization running full ward tickets, the club did not intend to extend its action beyond an effort to reform the schools by the election of women. This made it necessary to confine its canvass to the two women whom it had nominated. (See circular, "Women on School Boards," appended to this report.)

In order to make perfectly clear what was done, I will describe the ward as a whole. The Seventh Ward has for its northern boundary the south side of Spruce Street, for its southern boundary the north side of South Street, and for its eastern boundary the west side of Seventh Street, while its western boundary is the Schuylkill River. It has an area of 281 acres, or a little short of one-half a square mile. It contains, according to the United States census for 1890, 4750 houses. This area had in 1890, a population of 30,179, making it of about the average density for the city. As the inhabitants of the ward in 1880 were 31,080, the population has been practically stationary for fifteen years. The population in 1890 was one-third colored or 9002 all native. This leaves a white population of 21,177. Of this, one-third were foreigners or 6963, of whom 1000 were probably Russians and Poles. Of the remaining white population, born in this country, or 14,214 persons, one-half or 7324 were born of foreign parents. In other words, one-third the ward was colored and of the remaining two-thirds, one-third was of foreign birth, one-third was of foreign parentage and one-third was American. In the entire ward, a little short of one-fourth is of American white parentage. The ward, though in the centre of the city, has 4750 houses for its 5722 families, and 4083 families have each a separate house. This disposes of 20,400 of the population. Of the remaining 10,000, 5000 or 1002 families live in houses with two families each and only 639 live in houses with three or more families in a dwelling. In the entire ward there are only seventeen houses with six or more families apiece. House to house visiting in such a ward is practically visiting separate dwellings.

The school population in 1890, from five to twenty years of age was 8207; 5306 white and 2151 colored, born here, and 750 born abroad. There are about 5000 children from five to thirteen years of age inclusive, one-fourth colored. The ward has (see City School Report), thirteen schools and four kindergartens with sixty women and three men teachers, occupying five school buildings and two rented rooms. The schools in two of the buildings have been reorganized under supervising principals, making practically one school. There are also employed five housekeepers, all of whom are men.

With 5000 children who ought to be somewhere at school, the public schools held in 1880 an average attendance of 2561 and on December 31, 1894, 2490, a decrease of 71. In 1880, the enrollment was 2950 scholars; in 1894, 2442, a loss of 508 scholars. The children in the ward were no fewer. Apparently 1000 children in the ward do not go to public or private schools at all, and the number of such children has increased in the last fifteen years.

There were, I may add, in 1890, seventeen churches in the ward, assessed at $663,000, and fourteen charitable institutions, assessed at $715,000, so that as far as this ward is concerned, there are over a million and a quarter dollars devoted to religious and charitable work, general in character, but having a special responsibility to the ward. The valuation of the ward in 1893 was $22,000,000, about five per cent of the whole being devoted to charitable and religious objects, without including the schools; including the schools, I suppose it would amount to almost seven per cent.

The ward has along its eastern edge, a district composed largely of Italians and Russians, recently arrived in this country and living under unfavorable conditions. Along its western edge on the Schuylkill River, there is a district which has all that a semi-commercial river bank in a large city displays. Its larger and more valuable residences are along its northern boundary, and its southern boundary is devoted to small retail shops, supplying a large population of small householders.

The vote in the Seventh Ward for ten years (1884–1894) is as follows:

YEAR.	REPUBLICAN.	DEMOCRAT.	OFFICE.
1884	4222	1762	President.
1885	3097	1681	State Treasurer.
1886	3636	1446	Governor.
1887	3460	1568	State Treasurer.
1888	4590	1914	President.
1889	3634	1096	District Attorney.
1890	4373	1501	Governor.
1891	4003	1331	County Treasurer.
1892	4003	1361	President.
1893	3399	938	Judge of Supreme Court.
1894	4968	921	Governor.

The Republican majority in the ward is overwhelming, over five to one. An examination of the vote, as given above for a number of years, shows that the Democratic vote had fallen from 1762 to 921 in ten years; while the Republican vote during that time had advanced from 4222 to 4968.

The ward is divided into twenty-six election divisions. Each of these divisions is in the care of two Republican division workers who are responsible for the vote in their division; they are known as division bosses, and to them the money raised for use on election day, is given for distribution. In order to make perfectly clear the forces with which a canvass like ours has to contend, I have compiled a list of these fifty-two division workers, known as the Seventh Ward Union Republican Executive Committee, with the positions which they hold.

OFFICERS AND MEMBERS OF THE SEVENTH WARD UNION REPUB-
LICAN EXECUTIVE COMMITTEE.

OFFICERS.

President, Frank S. Harrison.
Vice-Presidents, James A. Russell, John Bishop, Stephen Frisby.

Recording Secretary, Wm. S. Smith.
Financial Secretary, Nathan Anderson. (Not in City Directory).
Treasurer, John C. Sheahan.
Member of City Committee, Israel W. Durham.

MEMBERS.

Division.

1 Joshua Evans, 706 Lombard Street. Billiards.
   George Hazzard, 720 Lombard Street. Billiards.

2 Nathan Anderson, 705 Minster Street. (Not in City Directory.)
   Laborer.
   Harry A. Scott, 729 Lombard Street. Liquor Dealer.

3 John C. Sheahan, 502 S. Ninth Street. Lawyer, City Collector's
   Office.
   Stephen Frisby, 932 Rodman Street. Watchman (not city).

4 James M. Waters, 1037 Barley Street. Employed at Public Buildings.
   Jacob Foreman, 1008 Barley Street. Employed at Public Buildings.

5 William P. Allmond, 1028 Lombard Street. Undertaker.
   Edward M. Gray, 1023 Rodman Street. Driver.

6 George B. Lewis, 1135 Ohio Street. Shoes. Lamp lighter.
   John F. Macken, 406 Quince Street. Clerk, Office Recorder
   of Deeds.

7 James A. Russell, 1214 Lombard Street. Clerk, Office Receiver
   of Taxes.
   Alfred Bettencourt, 1132 Lombard Street. Restaurant.

8 John Hunter, 410 S. Twelfth Street. Bricklayer. Gas Works.
   Samuel Jackson, 1213 Pine Street. Waiter.

9 B. F. Houseman, 403 S. Thirteenth Street. Bill Poster. Sheriff's
   Office.
   Frank Purnell, 1311 Ralston Street. Janitor, Surveyor's Office.

10 Edward C. Baxter, 519 S. Juniper Street. Sexton. Messenger, Harrisburg.
   Thomas Orr, 1328 Pine Street. Clerk, Water Department.

11 Samuel F. Houseman, 424 S. Broad Street. Select Councils.
   Daniel DeVinney, 1421 Lombard Street. Park Guard.

12 Clarence Meeser, 1531 South Street. (Not in City Directory.) Gas
   Works.
   Levi Oberton, 1534 Carver Street. Janitor, Office Receiver of
   Taxes.

Division.
13 William C. Loane, 532 S. Sixteenth Street. Segars. Water Depart-
     ment.
     Noble Harris, 1631 Lombard Street. Segars.
14 Frank S. Harrison, 421 S. Sixteenth Street. Magistrate.
     James Saunders, 1529 Pine Street. Waiter.
15 William Milligan, 1712 Burton Street. Foreman, Fire Department.
     John Philips, 1740 Lombard Street. Segars.
16 James F. Robinson, 1927 Wilcox Street. Bookkeeper.
     Edward Hanna, 329 S. Twentieth Street. Janitor, School House.
17 Israel Whitaker, 513 S. Nineteenth Street. Watchman, Walnut
     Street Bridge.
     William Hushwood, 1812 Naudain Street. Foreman, Fire De-
     partment.
18 William S. Smith, 1937 Watt Street. Clerk, Office Receiver of
     Taxes.
     David Frame, 1919 Naudain Street. Fireman.
19 Robert Hastings, 2021 Hampton Street. Clerk, City Treasurer's
     Office.
     William H. Patterson, 514 S. Twentieth Street. Sorter, Post
     Office.
20 Charles B. Hall, 2010 Pine Street. Sergeant-at-Arms, Common
     Council.
     John T. McConnell, 2012 Pine Street. (Not in City Directory.)
     Carpenter.
21 Charles H. Bennett, rear 429 South Albion Street. Ornamental
     Iron Worker.
     Edward Harley, 2136 Naudain Street. Fire Department.
22 David Winslow, 2209 Naudain Street. Water Department.
     George McKain, 2214 Naudain Street. Laborer, Gas Works.
23 William Larkey, 2419 Kent Street. Laborer, Gas Works.
     Patrick Morrissey, 2505 Pine Street. Laborer.
24 James Markey, 2405 Ashburton Street. U. S. Arsenal.
     Alexander Wray, 2701 Lombard Street. (Not in City Directory.)
     Foreman in coal yard.
25 W. J. Barton, 518 Barnwell Street. Captain, Almshouse.
     James McShane, 2608 Lombard Street. (Not in City Directory.)
     Employed at Almshouse.
26 William A. Mason, 1636 Pine Street. Clerk, Post Office.
     John Bishop, 1639 Helmuth Street. Watchman, Public Buildings.

The above list shows that the Republican working machine has in the ward:

1 Select Councilman.

1 Sergeant-at-Arms, Common Councils.

4 Employes, City Fire Department, 2 being foremen.

3 Employes of the Public Buildings.

4 Employes of the City Gas Works.

3 Employes of the City Water Department.

3 Employes of the Office of Receiver of Taxes.

2 Employes of the Post-Office Department.

1 Employe of the City Collector's Office.

1 Employe, Office of Recorder of Deeds.

1 Employe, Sheriff's Office.

1 Employe, U. S. Arsenal.

2 Employes, Almshouse.

1 Clerk of the City Treasurer's Office.

1 Watchman on Walnut Street Bridge.

1 Janitor of a school building.

1 Janitor of the Survey Office.

1 Park Guard.

1 Magistrate.

1 Lamplighter,

1 Messenger at Harrisburg.

—

35 in all, who are employed in city and Federal offices.

There are besides:

2 Segar Dealers.

2 Billiard Saloon Keepers.

1 Watchman.

1 Undertaker.

1 Driver.

2 Restaurant Keepers.

1 Moulder.

2 Waiters.

1 Bookkeeper.

1 Carpenter.

2 Laborers.

1 Foreman.

—

17 in all,

Who, together with the thirty-five above named, as employed in city offices, constitute the power which controls the schools by nominating yearly the School Directors through their conventions. Five of these names do not appear in the city directory.

The Democratic machine is of precisely the same character.

MEMBERS OF THE SEVENTH WARD DEMOCRATIC EXECUTIVE COMMITTEE.

Division.

1   Morris Hart, 707 South Street.   Clerk.

2   Frank S. Fagan, 400 South Eighth Street.   Clerk, Knickerbocker Ice Co.

Division.
3 James J. Devlin, 926 Pine Street. Cabinet Maker.
4 George P. Betton, 1017 Pine Street. Internal Revenue Department.
5 Henry Friend, 1021 South Street. Shoe Dealer.
6 Robert F. Simpson, 1104 Pine Street. "Gent."
7 Martin C. Kamp, 1237 South Street. Tinsmith.
8 James S. Holmes, 421 Dean Street. Janitor, Post Office.
9 Robert J. Owen, 1327 Pine Street. Clerk.
10 John Slevin, 504 South Thirteenth Street. Magistrate.
11 John H. Gaiton, 419 Wetherill Street. Salesman.
12 William Getty, 1509 South Street. (Not in Directory.) "Gent."
13 Dennis Boyle, 425 South Seventeenth Street. Blacksmith.
14 Michael Lydon, rear 315 Dugan Street. Expressman.
15 John McGettigan, 1715 South Street. Watchman, Surveyor's Office.
16 James V. Duffy, 322 South Nineteenth Street. (Not in Directory.) Dancing Master.
17 George P. Bickerton, 1834 Lombard Street. Plasterer.
18 Frank J. Pryor, Jr., 1919 Lombard Street. Clerk, U. S. Revenue Office.
19 John Bryson, 426 South Twentieth Street. U. S. Arsenal.
20 James Duffy, 405 South Twenty-first Street. Polisher.
21 Hugh J. O'Donnell, 420 South Twenty-first Street. Employed in Mint.
22 Thomas McBride, Jr., 2312 Lombard Street. Clerk.
23 Frank Quirk, 2535 Pine Street. Driver.
24 Patrick Morris, 2413 Ashburton Street. Driver.
25 Bernard J. Matthews, 512 South Twenty-fourth Street. Watchman.
26 Lawrence T. Lynch, 323 Bradford Street. Tailor.

The above list of names shows that the Democratic working machine has in the ward:

     1 Magistrate.
     1 Employe, Internal Revenue Department.
     1 Employe, U. S. Arsenal.
     1 Employe, U. S. Mint.
     1 Janitor, Post Office.
     1 Watchman, Surveyor's Office.
     1 Clerk, U. S. Revenue Office.

     7 in all, who are employed in city and Federal offices.

There are besides :

1 Cabinet Maker.	1 Plasterer.
2 " Gents."	1 Polisher.
1 Shoe Dealer.	2 Drivers.
1 Tinsmith.	1 Watchman.
1 Salesman.	1 Tailor.
1 Blacksmith.	1 Dancing Master.
1 Expressman.	—
4 Clerks.	19 in all,

Who, together with the seven above named, constitute the Democratic machine of twenty-six members, two of whom are not in the city directory.

If any of these politicians fail to keep up the regular Republican or Democratic vote in their divisions, they will at once lose their places.   I cannot give their salaries and receipts in detail, but I have no doubt they aggregate in all forms for the taxpayers of this city, fifty thousand dollars annually.   This is practically a corruption fund which is used to elect, among other officers, the School Directors, many of whom mismanage the schools of the ward, of which we have strong evidence.

In this past election we were practically beaten by the school board itself, whose members got together and said they would not allow a woman on the board, and directed their campaign work accordingly, with what success we already know.   The teachers in the schools of the ward also objected to women on school boards.   They therefore exerted all the influence possible by circulating the following petition among the parents, signed by fifty-four of the sixty-three teachers in the ward, requesting the citizens to vote for two of the candidates on the Republican ticket.   There were four candidates to be elected, each voter being only allowed to vote for three.   I leave you to draw your own conclusions.

PETITION OF PUBLIC SCHOOL TEACHERS OF SEVENTH WARD.

We, the undersigned teachers of the Public Schools of the Seventh Section, thoroughly impressed with the ability, integrity and zeal of Mr. S. K. Shedaker and Dr. E. Clarence Howard as school directors,

and their high moral standing as men, and believing that the best
interests of the schools of the section will be subserved by their reten-
tion in office, most earnestly and respectfully petition the honorable
citizens of the Seventh Ward, irrespective of creed or party, to cast, at
the coming election, their votes in favor of these gentlemen, who have
been tried and not found wanting.

In the face of this machine, the Civic Club set out to
persuade the voters of the ward to cast their ballots for their
two candidates.

Having described the manner of nomination, the ward
with its conditions and requirements, and that part of the
Republican machine which we had to fight, I will now ex-
plain the manner in which the work was done.

At the meeting of the Municipal Department on January
21, the chair appointed a committee to confer with the committee of the Educational Department, named on January
19, with Mrs. Mary E. Mumford as chairman, and Miss
Edith Wetherill as secretary.   These committees were to
meet at Mrs. Kirkbride's on January 22, to determine the
best method for securing the election of the two candidates
of the Civic Club, for the school board of the Seventh Ward.
The committee was given power to act.

This committee met, and after discussing various plans
appointed a special campaign committee, consisting of seven
women : Mrs. Thomas S. Kirkbride, Mrs. N. Dubois
Miller, Mrs. Lewis J. Parks, Mrs. Talcott Williams (chairman), Miss Edith Wetherill (secretary) and Miss E. K.
Carlile (assistant secretary), to which was afterward added
Miss Mary Channing Wister, in whose favor Mrs. Williams
resigned the chairmanship.   To Miss Wister's untiring
efforts, confined to her room, as she was, the greater part
of the time, is due a large share of whatever success the
work had.

This committee met on the morning of January 23, and
prepared the circular before alluded to, calling the joint
meeting of the two departments on the twenty-ninth, together
with all the Civic Club members residing in the ward,

and other women who would be willing to work for the cause. It apportioned the ninety-four members of the Civic Club residing in fifteen divisions of the Seventh Ward, to the twenty-six divisions of the ward, appointing a chairman for each division, and giving these chairmen power to call to their committees outside women up to the number of ten workers for each division. Finding it impossible to obtain Civic Club chairmen for more than eighteen divisions, six women from outside the club were persuaded to take charge of six divisions, several of whom have since become members of the club.

In two divisions, the fifth and the twelfth, there were no chairmen, the larger part of the work in the fifth having been admirably done by a paid worker, and that in the twelfth, by several women whose names will be found in the appended list of division workers. On January 29, the departments again came together to hear the plan of work briefly sketched, and to receive instructions. (The plan in detail is appended to this report.)

Assessors' lists, containing the names of all the voters in the ward, had been obtained from the County Commissioners' office at the City Hall. These had been cut up and pasted into twenty-six division books by Miss Carlile and her assistants and were then given to the chairman of each division, with instructions to note carefully against each name all information obtained. In each of these books a careful entry had been made on information obtained from the Charity Organization Society, as to houses which it was not deemed wise or prudent to visit for reasons which need not be enlarged upon. Duplicate lists were also furnished to each chairman to be cut up and distributed among the division workers. Printed instructions for the work were given to each chairman; also printed circulars entitled " Neighbors and Friends," with instructions to leave them at each house which was visited, pinning them up when allowed, in some prominent place in the room.

The division committees at once set to work with their house to house canvass. A series of parlor meetings on Spruce and Pine streets, including the adjacent cross streets, having been decided upon, also meetings in halls and churches, a program committee was appointed consisting of

Miss Florence Kane, Chestnut Hill ;
Miss Caroline Lewis, 250 S. Sixteenth Street ;
Mrs. J. Willis Martin, 1709 Walnut Street ;
Miss Ada Miles, 258 S. Eighteenth Street ;
Miss Matilda H. Morris, 137 N. Twentieth Street ;
Miss Edith Wetherill, Chalkley Hall ;

with Miss Mary Channing Wister as chairman, to arrange for meeting places and to obtain speakers. To facilitate the work of the meetings the twenty-six divisions were arranged in six groups, known respectively as groups A, B, C, D, E and F, hall meetings being held by these division groups. Of this work, the sixteen parlor meetings, the ten meetings held in halls, and the eight meetings held in churches, the three mothers' meetings and sewing circles addressed, Mrs. Kirkbride and Miss Wetherill will report.

These meetings, as with all political meetings, served the two purposes of informing the audience and showing for what manner of persons votes were asked. It was of priceless value at this stage of the work that Mrs. Kirkbride, one of the candidates, was able to speak impressively, effectively and eloquently, and to her speeches as well as to her happy way of receiving the many people who came to her, was due the favorable impression which the canvass made in the ward.

Letters were also sent to the clergymen of all the churches in the ward, asking them to give out from their pulpits the notices of meetings as sent to them. The clergymen of several of the colored churches, made '' Neighbors and Friends '' .the text of their sermons on the two intervening Sundays.

All circulars and notices of meetings were always sent to the Seventh Ward Charity Organization headquarters where Miss Burk and her assistants did most efficient work.

The campaign committee met every morning at Mrs. Kirkbride's, some of them being in attendance from ten to twelve
o'clock, to give information and distribute the literature to
the workers.

A second circular was issued entitled: "Unhealthy School
Houses," being a reprint from an article published in the
Philadelphia *Press*. Most of the workers made a second
visit to distribute these, as well as the notices of meetings to
be held in their groups of divisions.

To Miss Cornelia Frothingham's tireless work, early and
late, reading of proof at all hours, watching the printing of
circulars and notices, was due the promptness with which
they were always ready when needed, an indispensable matter in the rapid work of a canvass.

On February 12, the Educational and Municipal Departments of the club again met the chairmen of division workers.
Reports of the progress of the work were heard from twenty-
one of the twenty-six divisions. Five hundred badges,
presented by Mrs. J. Willis Martin, reading: "Women
Want Women on School Boards to Care for Their Children,"
were given to the chairmen for distribution, also the specimen
ballots, on the larger share of which the names of the two
candidates had been crossed under the Municipal League
caption. These were for distribution in the Republican divisions. On a few of the ballots the two names were crossed
under the Democratic caption. These were, of course, for
distribution in the Democratic divisions. These ballots
required another, and in some ways, more important visit to
be paid, as on its being understood how to cross correctly
the two names on the ballot, largely depended the success of
the canvass. There were about 5000 of these ballots distributed. (A copy, official size, is bound in with this report.)
To the chairmen were also given division maps of the
ward.

A most surprising amount of house to house work was
done throughout the ward, the division books showing that

almost every one of the 4750 houses had been visited, the larger share of them, three times, making in all some 13,000 visits which had been made by the division workers. The college settlement having a fuller acquaintance, before the canvass began, with its own division, the first, made a model report. Another model report was the following made by Mrs. William Krause of the third division:

THIRD DIVISION, SUMMARY.

Voters, Republican	214
Voters, Democratic	35
Voters, Uncertain	95
Fraudulent Names	61
Under age	17
Total	422
Total names on assessors' list	422

The result showed a very close canvass, as on election day in this third division there were 206 votes cast for the Republican candidate, and 74 votes for the Democratic and Municipal League candidate, 142 names on the list casting no ballot, of these names 78 were not entitled to vote, so that 8 of the uncertain ballots were cast for the Republican ticket and 23 for the opposition.

In the course of the house to house canvass, 960 names were discovered on the assessors' lists which had no business to be there. The knowledge that these names had been discovered in which the double canvass made by the Municipal League, greatly aided, undoubtedly prevented men from voting on these names, as there was much less repeating on election day than usual. The names of these presumably illegal voters arranged by divisions alphabetically, in separate books, were furnished by the committee to the watchers of the Municipal League for challenge on election day.

The difficult and laborious task of keeping the records of all the fraudulent entries as they were turned in, day by day,

by the division workers, and of compiling and arranging
from the window books for ready use, over 5000 names on
the assessors' lists and nearly 1000 fraudulent votes reported,
was patiently and skillfully discharged by Miss Carlile, for
whose work no praise can be too high.

Our meetings, our house to house canvass, our circulars
and our posters, drew an attention to our canvass which no
previous reform movement in the ward has ever received.
Defeated as we were, we forced every voter and every family
in the ward to stop and consider the condition of the
schools.

When election day came, the condition of the ward was
as follows: In all of the divisions except the twenty-fourth,
twenty-fifth and twenty-sixth, the Municipal League had
watchers and workers—sixty in all. Of these, nine were
men appointed at the request of the Civic Club committee,
and paid from the money given by the Committee of
Ninety-five, for a special election work. To its chairman, Mr. Rudolph Blankenburg, and to its members,
our grateful acknowledgments are due, for help at a critical
emergency.

In one division only—the second—was the Municipal
League allowed an overseer. Heretofore only the Republicans and Democrats have been granted overseers. But the
second division is so notoriously crooked that the court
granted an overseer to the Municipal League for that division. This overseer had been obtained by the Civic Club
committee, as had eight others, together with the affidavits
of five respectable residents in each of those divisions in which
overseers were needed, divisions where it was felt imperative
to have them, but the court refused to allow more than
this one. The result of the elections in these divisions
demonstrates the judgment of the committee to have been
right.

There are three sets of officials recognized at the polls.
In the first place, the judge and two inspectors, who are

known as election officers, and who are elected each February, to serve at all the elections during the ensuing year. Each inspector appoints one clerk, making five officials in each division. These officers are practically limited to the two political parties, so that a reform organization has no opportunity to be represented among them as there are three elected, and each voter is only allowed to vote for two. These officers sit inside the rail and are paid by the city treasurer.

Outside the rail is the second set of officials, consisting of the watchers, three being allowed from each organization represented on the ticket, but only one from each organization being allowed in the polling place at one time. The duties of a watcher consist in keeping poll or window books and challenge lists. They should not fail to exercise the right to challenge suspected voters, and should follow them up by requiring the necessary proofs to be furnished. They can act as helpers if necessary.

One watcher for each party or group may remain in the voting room, outside the rail, after the polls are closed, until the votes have been counted and the results announced. They are entitled to have an unobstructed view of the ballots while they are being counted, and should keep their eyes on the ballots from the moment they are taken from the box, until they are returned there and the box sealed.

The official appointment of watchers costs nothing. An application is made to the County Commissioners by the official representative of the ticket, on whose behalf the watchers are asked, and they issue certificates of appointment which must be shown to the election officers at the polls at 6.30 on the morning of the election. The watchers are not paid from the public treasury, but have to be paid by the representative of the ticket which they watch, as few men who are willing to stand from 6.30 a. m. until the count is concluded, oftentimes long after midnight, can afford to do so without pay. In some of the divisions of the Seventh

Ward in the last election the returns were not in until after
3 a. m.   It would mean to them the loss of one-sixth of their
weekly income.   The customary pay of a watcher is two
dollars per day.   This gives two sets of officers recognized
by law, one set inside the rail and another set outside the
rail.   The only way in which the Civic Club could secure its
own watchers, would be by having its own school director
ticket, which it could easily do another year.

When there is reason to believe the election officers are
bent on fraud or when they are all from one party, application
can be made to the court for overseers, who constitute the
third set of officials recognized at the polls.   An overseer can
watch every stage of the election from within the rail, and
keep his own list of the voters.   It is his duty to remain
within the rail until all the returns are completed and the
ballot box sealed.   If he has reason to think that a ballot
has not been properly counted, he has a right to note the
same on the back of the ballot.   An election officer refusing
to permit the overseer the full opportunity of discharging
his duty, is punishable by a fine of $1000 and imprisonment
for one year.   If the overseer is driven away or intimidated,
the whole poll of that election district may be set aside.   In
securing overseers, five affidavits from reputable residents of
the division are required by law for each overseer, and the
legal charge of the notary for obtaining these affidavits is
$1 for each, making the affidavits for each overseer cost $5.
The overseers receive $5 from the public treasury and it is
always customary for the representative of the party by
whom their appointment is secured to pay them $5 in addi-
tion, making the legal cost to the appointing party of each
overseer, $10.   To have had overseers at the polls of the
eleven divisions, in which the election officers were all Republican, as should have been done, would have cost $110.
Through the courtesy of notaries who were interested in the
election of women on school boards, we were charged, in most
cases, only the minimum price of fifty cents for each affidavit.

With the corrupt election officers, lies the chief cause of our corrupt elections. This can only be remedied by a strenuous and perhaps troublesome effort. The not doing is usually easier than the doing. If the best men of the ward would go to the primaries, which nominate the election officers, such men could not be nominated as the judge of the first division, who was released from jail, where he was imprisoned for hitting a man on the head with a hatchet, to judge his division in the election last November, and was again the judge of his division at the February election. It is the lowest men in the party who go to the primaries and make their undisturbed nominations of men of their own kind for election offices. So quietly is it all done and so underhandedly that the names of the election officers to be voted for at this last election were not put on the specimen ballots sent out before election day, and I was not able to find out who had been nominated in my own division, until I found the names on the specimen ballots required by law to be hung outside each polling place on election day. One hour, or at most two, given to the work of the primaries twice a year, by the honest, conscientious men of each division, would make some great changes for the better.

To my horror, I find on looking into the matter, I have twice had dinners on the night of the Republican primary in my own division. As it convenes at 7.30, I have therefore been responsible for keeping more than one Republican away. If the women of the Civic Club will take the trouble to look up the dates of the primaries which come for local offices early in January and in October, and are always published by law, in the newspapers, and will urge the men of their acquaintance to go to these primaries, more especially to the one in January, they can do much to secure the nomination of honest election judges.

Whatever else was accomplished, the canvass succeeded in bringing out a much larger vote than usual, as the following

vote by divisions for School Directors in the Seventh
Ward, February 19, 1895, shows:

Division.	Shedaker.	Esrey.	Howard.	Williams.	Kirkbride.	Sellers.
1 . . .	110	105	105	45	45	32
2 . . .	345	247	251	46	41	110
3 . . .	205	196	206	74	73	54
4 . . .	164	144	153	69	69	62
5 . . .	183	177	178	34	35	31
6 . . .	127	107	111	72	75	61
7 . . .	243	193	206	15	13	49
8 . . .	204	155	197	61	60	83
9 . . .	217	194	207	65	66	64
10 . . .	171	166	165	23	23	36
11 . . .	90	80	81	71	72	57
12 . . .	190	185	175	17	16	98
13 . . .	295	293	293	49	49	47
14 . . .	119	100	114	73	71	48
15 . . .	234	199	191	47	49	86
16 . . .	61	56	54	77	77	79
17 . . .	142	149	143	52	49	52
18 . . .	105	102	104	74	74	73
19 . . .	146	144	142	86	85	97
20 . . .	87	76	81	102	100	102
21 . . .	118	115	118	94	93	89
22 . . .	112	107	114	132	131	127
23 . . .	84	80	82	139	141	132
24 . . .	88	88	86	89	88	88
25 . . .	122	121	122	77	75	83
26 . . .	153	194	137	27	26	64
	4115	3773	3816	1710	1701	1904

In the first place the opposition vote at the November election was 900. This time it was 1904, the largest opposition
vote ever polled in this ward, and the only ward in the city
in which the opposition vote polled was larger than usual at
this election. The vote for the two women was 1710 and
1701 respectively, but it was their vote which raised the vote
cast for the third candidate to 1904. In some divisions both
the vote and the count were fair and the women received all
promised to them.

In the first division two of the election officers were notoriously corrupt. On the Monday before election, Mrs. Kirkbride received a postal from one of them stating that he
" could be seen at his place of business until election day."
This offer clearly can have but one construction. A ward
worker in another division offered to sell out his division for
$50.

In the fourteenth division, when the polls closed, the
election officers sat down, refusing for two hours to begin
counting the vote, thinking they could tire out the watchers,
when there would be an opportunity to count the vote as
might best please them. At the end of two hours, finding
our watchers could out-sit them, they proceeded with the
count. The following was the watched result:

Williams 73,
Kirkbride 71,
Sellers 48.

Mr. Sellers ran 194 votes ahead of the highest vote cast
for either of the women candidates. This plurality was
secured in the second division, where he obtained sixty-four
votes more, in the eleventh division where he obtained eighty-
one votes more, and in the fifteenth and in the sixteenth divisions in each of which he secured thirty-seven votes more.
The condition of the second has already been mentioned.
The twelfth is notoriously one of the worst divisions in the
ward, and the fifteenth and the sixteenth divisions are nearly
as bad. In all these divisions the Democratic vote is so
small, that it need scarcely to be considered. Mr. Sellers
was elected by the aid of his Republican friends, who pre-
ferred the candidate of the Democratic machine to women
who were pledged to the reform of the schools and to justice
to all classes.

In the Democratic divisions the entire Democratic vote
was honorably cast for both the woman candidates, and all
the obligations of a nomination were fully met. At the
same time there was no doubt from the start that the

Republican machine intended to aid the selected Democratic candidate.

On election day, the two Civic Club candidates with two division workers and an officer of the Municipal League, made the complete round of the twenty-six polling places of the Seventh Ward, and were treated throughout with entire courtesy. Whatever their political conduct may be, the election officers and others at the polls had not forgotten that they were Americans. It was pleasant, with so much else that one must condemn, to find that the American citizen had not lost his traditional courtesy to women. I am told that thirty or forty years ago, rioting at the polls was so rife, that such a trip would not have been possible. More than one murder was often reported the next morning, in connection with the election returns of the city.

Throughout the preliminary work in arranging for the protection of the interests of the Civic Club candidates at the polls, the committee received priceless assistance, advice and encouragement from Mr. Charles Henry Jones, whose long efforts for pure elections in the Fifth Ward constitute one of the brightest pages in its dark political history.

The Seventh Ward presents every difficulty which it is possible to find, from the apathy of the better educated; many of whom will not take the trouble to pay their poll tax, to the ignorance of a large part of the population.

The wealthier part of the ward has only a platonic interest in the public schools. Its members do not send their children to these schools, as under their present political management no parents will send their children to them if they can send them to better schools. The most moral and conscientious Catholics send their children to their own parochial schools. The only class of which the religious and moral portion interest themselves in the public schools, are the colored population, because they send their children to them, and are obliged to do so, or keep them at home, none of the private schools admitting them.

The greatest aid and assistance was received from Mrs. Fannie Coppin, who for many years has led the cause of education for the colored people in this city. Special acknowledgment is due to the colored clergymen of the ward who, under strong political pressure, showed a courage, zeal and readiness to appeal to their flocks on reform issues, which deserves a wide and general imitation.

We have failed in our assault, and the question of future success turns on whether we are willing to undertake a siege. Why did we fail in the assault? First—because the organization was opposed to us. Second—our lack of acquaintance with the voters. Third—our failure to persuade the people that women would really manage the schools better than men. A fourth reason why we failed is because the large part of the voters in the ward felt that they had more confidence in the men who had taken the trouble to make their acquaintance before they asked for their vote, than in the women whom they had not known until they asked for their vote.

We must all remember that superior education, information or refinement, confers no privilege to direct education. It only creates obligation and responsibility to serve the public by slowly educating it.

The machine has always in every division, two or three men who all the year around are keeping up relations with the voters, obtaining, for instance, through the ward bosses, for men out of work, places on the traction lines and on the railroads, helping to get their children transferred from school to school, and organizing political clubs whose rent and expenses are met by the office holders. There are besides the corrupt influences at work, such as payments on election day, obtaining discharge after arrest for some petty crime, and protection of the "speak-easies." In addition, these men look after all the political details of their divisions, they know every voter, at least by sight.

The watchers of the machine were selected long before

election day ; those of the Municipal League were appointed at the eleventh hour.

The *corrupt* part of the business of the machine, of course we cannot do, but is there any reason why each of us should not take the division in which she lives, and make it a point before the next election to know all about it ? If there is trouble, sickness or death in the little row of houses which are at the back of almost every one of our dwellings, it ought to be understood that the Civic Club representative is the best person in the division to go to. This representative ought to get into relations with the Charity Organization Society, investigate cases in the division, and distribute its relief. A perfect charity organization would have a competent woman in every division looking after its cases. Such a division representative would know what church their neighbors attended, and establish relations with the clergymen—white or colored, Protestant or Catholic.. With tact, with care to avoid offence, something further would be learned about every house in the division and the voters, and every effort would be made through the year to prepare for an appeal in January and February for the right vote.

Very nearly the best work in the canvass was done by the young women of the college settlement. Is there any reason why each of us should not turn her own home into a college settlement for the benefit of those around us who need help?

If an organization like this is extended over the city by the women of the Civic Club, as could be done by patient effort through several years, it would be entirely possible to take the schools out of politics.

So far as I am concerned, I am ready to take the fourteenth division of the Seventh Ward, and I will be glad to co-operate in an attempt to reorganize the ward now, for the next February school board election; but it will be useless to do this unless enough women are willing patiently to do this work in every division.

331 South 16th St.   SOPHIA W. R. WILLIAMS.

PERSONAL ASPECTS OF THE CANVASS.

At the beginning of the second year of the Civic Club two of its departments were found in active co-operation, carrying on a non-partisan campaign in which many members of the other two departments took an active share. That a four-fold organization, so early in its history, after a year's work on four distinct lines, should thus suddenly discover the perfect harmony of its parts, the co-ordination of its powers, was of itself an achievement. No apple of discord, but a "consummate flower" of unity, is to-day the first fruits of the initiative political work of the Civic Club.

It is proposed to supplement what has gone before by a review of some of the events of the campaign, and to glance at certain of its aspects not already noticed. The Seventh Ward encloses in its limited area unnumbered municipal problems; and within it are all the forces that purify and perpetuate, as well as all those that tend to destroy, a city's life. Although, of course not in every sense, representative, it would yet be hard to find a more complete type in miniature of the American city of our time.

It has its good things, many of which could be made better: homes, schools, churches, charities, hospitals—three of the last, where medical science, applied with all the ambition and devotion of doctor and of nurse, often fails to remedy the bodily ills that pure water, clean streets and enlightened liquor laws could easily prevent. Like all large American cities, this ward has not only good, but great things also—the Pennsylvania Hospital, that old foundation, and the newer glory of the Pennsylvania Museum and School of Textile Art.

It has its bad things, some of them so irretrievably bad, they ought now to be ground to powder, while some demand re-birth or new development; but as they now stand they

(39)

are all bad—saloons, low theatres, which little children frequent unattended, sweat-shops, dance-halls, dives, houses
that look outwardly like homes, but are not.   It is almost
useless to add that it has no amusement hall, where boys
and girls of the poorer classes can gather with their parents,
for elevating entertainment, and no park as breathing place,
although the wretchedness of its slums is a by-word.

Turning to men, this Seventh Ward is still more typical.
It has no banking or business houses, no large stores; but
men representing these interests live within it.   All its
political influence is centred in a long-existent and powerful
"Boss," his machine in perfect working order.   Yet
here live all kinds of citizens, the young men and the
middle-aged, crowded with work, but eager for reform, the
old men with public spirit unquenched; two of them
weighted with more than ninety years—one must speak
their names—Wm. H. Furness and Frederick Fraley—went
to the polls in February and voted for the women.   Here
live men alike capable of crime against the ballot, whom
outward circumstance separates widely: the intelligent and
affluent, who neglect all civic duty; the ignorant and de-
praved, who sell or barter votes.   Of both these classes, it
has unfortunately a large contingent.

It is the home of some of Philadelphia's most earnest and
independent colored citizens, but they are far outnumbered
by others whom the machine controls.   A large floating
colored population drawn, each winter from the South, by
false hope of employment, adds to the facilities for corruption.   To sum up, the Seventh Ward, in city parlance, is
notoriously a bad ward.   Was it by mere accident, that in
such a ward was carried on the first strictly political work
ever attempted by women in Philadelphia, and that from it
nearly one quarter of the members of the Civic Club
report ?

The story of the campaign properly begins with the un-
expected moment, when through a personal call from the

Chairman of the Seventh Ward Municipal League Committee, each candidate received notice of her nomination.

Shortly afterward, the candidates, by invitation of the Ward Municipal League Committee, met the other nominees upon the ticket. This was possibly the first invitation extended to women in Philadelphia to meet, as candidates, other candidates for city office. This friendly overture showed the desire of the Municipal League Committee, that the women candidates with the Civic Club behind them, should for the time be fully identified with the interests of the Municipal League party. It was, however, wisely decided, that in the event of an active campaign, the Civic Club and the women candidates should represent only the great principle of the need of women in the supervision of school affairs.

Two courses now lay open. Defeat was virtually certain; it could be awaited with folded hands or resolutely met, and duty perhaps called women to lay claim to that share of direction in the public schools which the law had so long sanctioned.

The latter course would demand all the time and energies of the candidates until the election, the unselfish aid of a large corps of helpers, the support of the Civic Club as an organization, and from individual members a contribution of several hundred dollars to cover the cost of a campaign. The feeling of the club was fully tested. It was ready for action, the president at once heading the subscription list with her gift of $50, and the work proceeded on the lines described by Mrs. Williams.

The scenes at the headquarters, which was open at all hours, have been already referred to. Here, for more than three weeks, from 10 a. m. to 10 p. m., one or both secretaries were constantly employed. While one candidate as organizer and executive, was unceasingly engaged in active and varied work, the other had the simpler offices of addressing the meetings and receiving workers in her home. The largest number of visitors on any one day was about forty, but constantly from twelve to twenty came in during the day for instructions or supplies of the printed matter, so largely in demand. Miss Wister's illness removed her share of un-intermitted work to her house and often to her room, thus lessening the activity at the headquarters. Miss Frothing-ham added the entire supervision of the campaign printing to the pressure of her usual duties.

The intense cold of the weeks beginning February 3, when the thermometer sank to zero, did not chill the ardor of the canvass, and much good work was accomplished during those trying days. Gentlewomen shrink from entering the houses of strangers, on an unusual errand, unbidden. This feeling disappeared before the civic zeal which lead women, representing the best that life can give in education and refine-ment, to ask admission to every home on the assessors' lists.

One fact was plain, usually the easiest, possibly the best, canvassing was accomplished when two workers went to-gether. There is undoubtedly psychological reason for send-ing out laborers, who strive to influence action through new thought, by two and two. Canvassing was not easy nor even agreeable to all. To a few it proved distasteful and was unsuited; but many workers, and some of these were well acquainted with philanthropic service, found this work the broadest and the most inspiring they had ever touched.

Early in the campaign, a nucleus of interest was sought among the educated colored residents of the ward; as a result of a conference held with some of the cultivated colored women living in or near it, Mrs. Fannie Coppin, formerly of Oberlin College, and for many years head of the Friends' In-stitute for Colored Youth, threw her large influence in favor of women directors. Other women as division chairmen and workers showed equally practical sympathy. Special meet-ings were held in chapels, and at larger meetings called for other objects the subject was given full hearing. Mrs. Coppin, to use her own expression, was one evening permitted "to capture" for a few minutes a congregation numbering 1500.

Possibly, could we read the future, it would be seen that for other ends besides those directly aimed at, women of the colored and the white race were thus unexpectedly drawn together during the Seventh Ward canvass, and some of the latter made conscious of great forces for political good, so near them, and yet before these campaign weeks, practically unknown.

The parlor meetings were as a rule more useful in strengthening and enlarging the views of converts, than in bringing scoffers into the righteous ways that lead women to school boards. They were especially valuable for the light thrown, by the frequent addresses of Miss Hallowell and Mrs. Mumford, upon the subject which so closely concerns us all, the true education of the children in the city's schools. The many public meetings were carried out with varying success in attendance, but with unvarying success in practical suggestions for future effort on the same lines. Busy men and women, summoned often at shortest notice by the Program Committee, were most responsive. Well known men, the best speakers in Philadelphia, turned from a multiplicity of engagements to raise their voices in the cause.

The good order at the public meetings failed only once. This exception was singularly instructive. Two men, the one made combative, fortunately only in words, and the other declamatory by liquor, broke in constantly upon the proceedings. The latter twenty times during the meeting, raising his right arm, emphatically affirmed by it, that he would carry his division " for the ladies "—and he did. The pugnacious individual with querulous questions, suggested by, but somewhat foreign to the subject under discussion, at intervals interrupted the speakers—only the men, however—strangely enough the women were heard in silence. Yet the meeting was a great success—the interest of the audience was thoroughly sustained, and best of all, a young mechanic pronounced it the next day, " one of the most entertaining lectures he had ever attended." Surely this is an important

hint, upon which the Civic Club might well take action. If
the subject of "Women on School Boards" was made so
pleasing, it may be practicable at other than election times
to hold attractive meetings, and thus awaken interest on
many municipal questions, besides giving much needed entertainment, and setting up rivalry to the political delights
of the saloon.

Two characteristic meetings were held in the College Settlement Hall, where the night before election, a large audience gathered, drawn by the music of a brass band, specially
engaged for the occasion. The Davis Cadets, a corps of boys
from the poorest quarters brought to new life under the care
of the Settlement, gave wide-awake attention to the speakers.
They wore the campaign badge, which we must believe,
hereafter, will become an historic emblem. "This year,"
said one small prophet, pointing to his badge, "it is 'Women
want Women on School Boards,' next year it will be 'Men
want Women on School Boards.'" Another, turning eagerly
to a son of one of the candidates, exclaimed, "You'll vote
for the women; you won't go back on your mother." What
a challenge this, flung out by this young champion in the
slums, not to the Seventh Ward only, but to all the city's
voters. When will the men of Philadelphia cease to "go
back" upon their mothers and their wives, and holding fast
to the practical ideas of women, work persistently to win for
us and for themselves, good city government?

The candidates attended by invitation three of the Satur-
day evening Municipal League meetings, presenting their
claims at each. At these meetings, as at those called by the
Campaign Committee, the lack of intelligence in the faces
of many of the men, who yet had enough interest in politics
to be present, shows that the intelligence of women ought at
once to be exerted in providing means to develop that of ignorant voters. The following incident is to the point: A
young colored man, member of a Sunday School class, when
his teacher regretted that he lived in the Eighth Ward, and

therefore could not vote for her friend as director, answered,
"Wouldn't your lady friend have my vote? Wouldn't she
like it? Why I could just walk over into the Seventh Ward
and vote there? What difference does it make if I do live
in the Eighth Ward?"

It has already been stated that the opposition excited by
the activity of the canvass, repeating similar experiences in
other cities, centred in the school board and teachers. It
may be added that each candidate received a call of protest
from a teacher who remarked, that she couldn't understand
why any woman could want to get a place as school director.
Her attitude differed from that of an old family servant, who,
when asked by a friend of the family to vote for the women
candidates, thought a while, and consenting, said, "Two
ladies can't do much harm anyway." Some years ago women candidates ran in the Ninth Ward. An article published at the time opposed their election on the ground that
"Women cannot understand the feelings of fathers." In
reflecting on the opposition of the Seventh Ward school
board we can only re-echo this sentiment.

The campaign was not without humorous episodes. Some
of these caused melancholy thought to women made abnor-
mally serious, by continued privilege of tax-paying without
representation. Urgent request was made by a supposed in-
timate of the editor of a small paper for an article on the
school question. It was written and sent. Then appeared
the editor asking the meaning of the article sent without
signature, and an editorial already in proof, warning against
the women candidates, was shown, proper explanation, however, might prevent its publication. Met by calm words, not
ready money, the editor left in haste to meet another en-
gagement.

The following sentences are taken from a letter received
from a member of a political club of colored men:

. . . I have speared no pains in putting fourth every effort
possible for the comeing event. . . . I am proud to say that

the good citizens of the *sixth division* and Seventh Ward . . . vows to cast their vote for you on the day of the election. I not only think for a moment that the *sixth division* alone will vouch for you, but so far as I have learned the whole entire ward is appealing to the lady *candidates* of this *ward* for good discipline and the education of the young. I am sure I can see nothing to prevent you from carrying the victory in this fight. I will do all I can as I will be around the polls and I know with the expenditure of a little money I can carry many my way. And my way is for you to win. . . .

The letter was followed the next day by a call from its urbane writer.

Late in the afternoon, the day before the election, a four-wheeler stopped at headquarters, its occupant, a colored man with a decided turn for politics, an errand runner in a market and very impecunious. He alighted and awaited the candidate's return. She was thus accosted on the sidewalk, ''I have come to tell you only two men in the ward can be trusted, they are the only ones who are true to you.'' With this alarming announcement, he returned to the cab, which was driven rapidly away. In an hour it returned with two occupants; the candidate was summoned to her door: '' Here,'' said the former speaker, pointing to his companion, while a strong odor of whiskey filled the vestibule, '' here is one of the two men I spoke to you about, I've brought him to tell you *he* is faithful and trustworthy.'' The ungrateful candidate was not moved to pay for the privilege of looking at such devotion.

The day before the election came the postal from the election judge, mentioned by Mrs. Williams. He is certainly a poor judge of the attitude of this club toward elections.

On election day, February 19, five members of the Civic Club accompanied the chairman of the Seventh Ward Municipal League committee in his visits to the polls. It was necessary to see that all watchers engaged were at their posts, and that each of the twenty-six boys sent out early with banners inscribed in large letters, '' Remember your Children and Vote for Women on the School Board,'' was duly on duty at his poll.   The sun shone brightly on the icy pavements, and as the day went on made dampness damper, the bricks under foot reeked with moisture.   The piles of snow beside the trolley track were black with city grime.   The alleys, uncleaned because the law requires that they must become nuisances and be reported as such to the Board of Health before cleansing, were choked with hillocks of snow variegated with refuse.   Never did Lombard and South streets look dirtier or appeal more visibly for woman's help.

It was probably the first time that a group of earnest women had ever systematically visited the voting places of the ward.   Their presence, as they stood for a few minutes near each poll, was observed at first with mute amazement, then with evident recognition of the fact that women had personal interest in the day's results.   They met with no discourtesy; frequently with kindly and respectful greeting. The following day, one newspaper, however, had a short article headed '' Women Hustle for Votes,'' beginning thus: ''A feature of the election in the Seventh Ward was the hustling canvass made by the women, who, accompanied by Lincoln L. Eyre, went from division to division throughout the ward, urging the voters to cast their ballots for the Municipal League candidates for school directors.''   It is needless to say that no votes were asked for.

In one place words ran high and knives were drawn, when the chairman of the League entered the narrow hall leading directly to the polling booth.   It was not his division, and a half-drunken man objected, inciting others. The other polls, when visited, were free from disorder. With the above exception, the effects of liquor were not noticeable until the afternoon, when it became evident that saloons were open, though their doors were closed.

In the division next to that poll, where a narrow hall was crowded by angry brawlers, the broad entrance of a school house looked morally advantageous, and seemed a model polling place. Three men were passing through the court, and one, in answer to inquiry, replied that for many years the polls had been held there, the children of one section of the school therefore had a holiday at each election, and the city was thus saved twenty-five dollars. He knew this, he was himself an election officer. At the moment just preceding this conversation, one of the party of women heard this officer say to the other white man, while pointing to their colored companion: '' Take him across the street and give him a drink.'' School houses as polls may not prevent all irregularities, and possibly the loss to the children of a day's schooling was scarcely made up by the twenty-five dollars saved the city.

Some of the polls, especially one held in an unrented shop, with large windows directly on the street, gave good opportunity to scan the faces and note the appearance of the election officers. On that day in the Seventh Ward, true citizens of all classes performed self-sacrificing duty at the polls, and there is possibility, too, of worth disguised by outward looks; but the eye cannot always deceive, and it was painfully apparent that almost all the men in authority at the polls fell far below the standard which ought to be demanded in officials elected for such important service.

As is apt to happen when women start on a new mission, unlooked-for occupation came. One of the company chanced at the first stopping place to hold two badges in her hand. A child asked for one, and was, of course, followed by another little beggar. The hint was acted upon, a large supply was brought. The badges which had hitherto been far less popular than the printed literature of the campaign, rose to unprecedented value, at every poll eager boys and girls rejoiced in the decoration.

In the first division the poll was surrounded by a group
of young colored men, whose looks showed the degradation
of the neighboring slums.   One of them, after watching the
satisfaction of the children, asked a badge for himself. The
request was taken up by others, their faces telling the same
tale of poverty and evil.

It was but a moment's task to pin a badge upon each
soiled and tattered coat, but what if responsibility rests upon
us women for such early shipwrecked manhood?

A happier reminiscence accompanies the thought of
another polling place in a western division, where a group
of a dozen children crowded about one of the party, and
detained her.   On looking back, the candidate, whose clear
brain had planned, whose unwearying energy had followed
every step of the campaign, was seen a very image of charity
bending over the little children, teaching, through the gift
of the campaign badge, a first civic lesson.

There remains only a glimpse of the dreary Municipal
League headquarters, where in the evening the tired watchers
gathered after long service at the polls.   Towards midnight
the special watchers, who had waited for the count in each
division, began to come singly, and as it seemed at long
intervals, each one reporting with eager haste the day's results.   In one division, where scratched tickets abounded,
and the count was long, an annoyed Republican inspector
exclaimed: "The women have done this."

The next day brought certainty of defeat, but no discour-
agement, and the Civic Club may well take up the words of
the Italian statesman, who, when taunted with political defeat, replied: "I call myself to-morrow."   Women will not
sit on the Seventh Ward school board during the coming
twelvemonth, but no machine management can drive them
from the outlook gained by this year's experience.   In any
real struggle for progress, defeat is never entire defeat, and
no victory ultimate.   Were all the reforms we long for accomplished to-morrow, at that very moment new paths of

imperative endeavor would open. We have been defeated, but what of the gain in learning for ourselves the sacrifice of time, the expenditure of strength and energy, the knowledge of affairs and the perseverance needed even in a small political venture? What of the gain in knowing something about the financial side of politics, and learning that much money must be raised and used, though strict economy controls expenses, and perfect honesty makes payments?

Is there no gain in realizing through the remembrance of wearied head and tired feet, and days preternaturally long, why men taxed to the utmost, in bread-winning, or engrossed by professional and business cares, or enamored of society or study, do not throw themselves into election or other work for good city government? Is there no gain in learning something of the chief race problem in our midst? What of the profit, too, in learning that even the restoration of the primaries to purity, conscientious voting for the best candidates, and a lively interest in elections will not of themselves fully accomplish ward regeneration.

The experience of one campaign forces the conviction, that back of all political organization lies that essential primary whose choices affect the body politic for good or ill, the unit of the value of each man's personality. There is but one sure and royal road to the purification of one bad ward, or to the good government of thirty-seven wards. Women are even now called to point it out, and will soon, if they prove equal to the task, be leaders upon the highway of human brotherhood. Already women begin to understand that the great principle of government of the people, by the people, for the people, has not caused misrule in our large cities. Misrule has come, because American citizenship has failed to grow with the growth of cities. The average citizen is now too small, too much dwarfed by personal interests, to see in human brotherhood the only true, working political force for his city and his ward.

From the beginning of the campaign some of those most active in it were impressed with a sense that an unseen power had called to the work, preparing it for them and them for it; the special capacity of each one fitting her for her special task. "Coincidences" beneath which, it is said Oliver Wendell Holmes felt "there is often a profound spiritual law which we do not now comprehend," were constantly about them. The same feeling recurred, when after writing the previous paragraphs, the concluding part of Mrs. Williams' paper was read by the present writer. The candidates of the late campaign, unknowingly to each other, through its review, have come to one conclusion. For what is the action to which Mrs. Williams urges us but the practical carrying out of the idea of human brotherhood? She has turned aspiration into possible reality. I, for one, am ready in the eleventh division, to answer to her call.

ELIZA B. KIRKBRIDE,

1406 Spruce Street.

REPORT ON OFFICE WORK, MEETINGS
AND SPEAKERS.

It is difficult to give a clear, short, business account of the office work, because there was too much done in a short time to keep very systematic records. There were letters to be written to members of the Civic Club living in the ward, to members of the Civic Club living outside the ward, and finally to any woman in the city who might be willing to help in the house to house visiting. There were speakers to be secured, there were invitations to parlor meetings to be sent out, there were two sets of twenty-six window books to be made up, and some members of the Campaign Committee were always in the office to act as a general bureau of information.

At Mrs. Kirkbride's invitation the committee made her house its headquarters, and there the work of the campaign was principally done. There the committee met the division chairmen and workers who came to get fresh supplies of campaign literature, notices of meetings, etc., and to compare notes about their visiting. The drawing room was completely metamorphosed, the piano did duty as a table to hold the leaflets, notices and appeals to our "Neighbors and Friends," a new ornament appeared on the wall near the door in the shape of a blackboard on which each morning were pinned notices of the meetings for the day; while the adjoining room was devoted to the assistant secretary, Miss Carlile, and her aids who made up the books in which were pasted the assessors' lists, and later the books containing the lists of fraudulent and erroneous names which were used by the watchers at the polls. When in sending out invitations to parlor meetings it became necessary to employ a typewriter, another room was given up to her use for five days, while two other professional workers were called in for three days and a half before the election.

The meetings above referred to were called in different parts of the ward, while the house to house visiting was being done, and were held in public halls, in churches and in private parlors. From the fifth to the nineteenth of February, thirty-three meetings were held in all.

PUBLIC MEETINGS IN HALLS.

Two at Y. M. C. A. rooms, 1120 Pine Street.
Tradesmen's Hall, Twenty-second and South Streets.
O'Neil's Hall, 1352 Lombard Street.
Magnolia Hall, Sixteenth and Lombard Streets.
Two at College Settlement, Seventh and Carver Streets.
Home for the Homeless, 708 Lombard Street.
Two at St. Luke's Guild, St. Luke's Church.

MEETINGS IN COLORED CHURCHES.

Church of the Crucifixion, pastor, Rev. L. G. Jordan.
Two at Bethel Chapel, pastor, Rev. W. D. Cook.
Wesleyan Church, pastor, Rev. F. H. Stitt.
Rev. Mr. Tallifiero's Sunday School, 1842 Lombard Street.
Two at Allen Chapel, Rev. W. H. H. Butler.

PARLOR MEETINGS.

Mrs. Wm. Rotch Wister (2), 1104 Spruce Street.
Mrs. Morris Longstreth, 1416 Spruce Street.
Mrs. Persifor Frazer, 928 Spruce Street.
Mrs. Theodore M. Etting, 1219 Spruce Street.'
The Misses Paul, 903 Pine Street.
Mrs. P. H. Brice, 1537 Pine Street.
Mrs. Robert P. Kane, 1024 Clinton Street.
Mrs. N. F. Mosselle, 1432 Lombard Street.
Mrs. Perry Johnson, 315 Dean Street.
Mrs. Samuel M. Fox, 339 S. Broad Street.
Mrs. C. N. Thorpe, 1729 Pine Street.
Mrs. Thomas Musgrove, Twentieth and Spruce Streets.
Mrs. Lincoln L. Eyre, 2302 De Lancey Street.
Mrs. William H. Ingham, 2134 Pine Street.
Miss Julia F. Jones, 1524 Lombard Street.

There were about 1250 invitations to the parlor meetings typewritten and sent out, and 25,900 printed notices of public meetings distributed, similar to the following:

WOMEN ON SCHOOL BOARDS!

PUBLIC MEETING,

Tuesday, February 12th,

at 3 o'clock,

ST. MARY STREET COLLEGE SETTLEMENT,

617 Carver Street.

COME AND BRING YOUR FRIENDS.

Addresses by the Women Candidates for the Seventh Ward School Board and other speakers.

These notices of the public meetings which were especially for the smaller streets, were printed on bright-colored paper and were left at the houses by the division visitors, who drew special attention to them; but though the people seemed interested in them at the time, the attendance at the meetings was very small.

As a suggestion for future work it may be well to note that people can often be induced to go to places with which they are familiar—as we found in the case of the colored churches—when they will not go to a strange place. The thanks of the committee are especially due to the colored clergymen who not only gave us the use of their churches, but in several cases spoke for us.

Notices for the parlor meetings were sent to each house within a few squares of the place of meeting, so that no one could plead distance as an excuse for not attending, but the citizens did not turn out in greater force on the large streets than on the small ones. Those who did come, however, showed a real and helpful interest. The sentiment of all the parlor meetings is best summed up by the following resolutions passed at the meeting at Dr. Persifor Frazer's house:

"*Whereas*, The question of the appointment of school commissioners is and ought to be in all civilized communities totally separated from the questions which agitate and divide great political parties.

Whereas, The proper care and guidance of the young is most safely entrusted to those persons who are outside of the baneful influences of partnership, and whose circumstances and surroundings produce a natural aptitude for a trust of this kind.

Whereas, The uninterrupted experience of twenty-five years in England, Germany, and a large and rapidly increasing number of the States of this country shows that the kind of women who are without exception nominated for such positions, have been those most success-ful in filling them.

Whereas, The candidates proposed for these positions are especially worthy of selection.

Therefore be it resolved, That we earnestly commend to the voters of this district without distinction of party Mrs. Thomas Kirkbride and Mrs. Talcott Williams for election as members of the school board."

But though the attendance at the meetings would scarcely average twenty at the public and twelve at the parlor meet-ings, the committee did not feel discouraged, for the notices and invitations advertised the movement, and we soon found that people were beginning to discuss the question among themselves, even if they did not care to hear us discuss it.

The chairman of the Campaign Committee, Miss Mary Channing Wister, was indefatigable in arranging meetings and securing speakers, but was prevented by illness from doing any more active work.

In acknowledging their obligations to all who helped in the campaign, the committee desire to express their heart-felt thanks to the speakers for the effort they made in behalf of the canvass, often at great personal inconvenience.

The following is a list of the speakers :

Dr. James MacAlister,	Rev. S. D. McConnell, D. D.,
Mr. Robert C. Ogden,	Miss L. A. Kirby,
Mr. Talcott Williams,	Mrs. N. F. Mosselle,
Miss Anna Hallowell,	Rev. Leverett Bradley,
Hon. John S. Durham,	Miss Katherine Bement Davis,

Mrs. J. P. Mumford,
Mrs. Fannie Coppin,
Mr. Joseph G. Rosengarten,
Dr. Morris Jastrow, Jr.,
Mrs. John H. Scribner,
Mr. Wm. M. Salter,

Mr. Rodman Paul,
Dr. Persifor Frazer,
Mrs. Cornelius Stevenson,
Mrs. N. Dubois Miller,
Mr. David Wallerstein,
Dr. Thos. G. Morton.

EDITH WETHERILL,
Secretary Campaign Committee.

Chalkley Hall, Philadelphia.

REPORT OF THE CIVIC CLUB CAMPAIGN FUND.

RECEIPTS.

From club contributions $373.25

EXPENSES.

Printing circulars	$75.90
Printing ballots	54.58
Wages of stenographer	46.80
Rent of typewriter	5.00
Messenger boys	26.29
Banner boys	19.00
Flags	15.00
Posters	7.50
Bill Posters	6.00
Perambulator	7.00
Wagon	3.00
Band	12.00
Canvassing	5.00
Watchers	3.00
Hall, College of Physicians	10.00
" Broad and Lombard Streets	2.00
" Thirteenth and Lombard Streets	2.00
Janitor's fee	1.00
Stationery, stamps, etc.	21.73

322.80

Balance . . . . $ 50.45

FRANCES CLARK,
Treasurer.

2008 DeLancey Place.

REPORT OF CAMPAIGN FUND FROM COMMITTEE OF '95.

RECEIPTS.

From Committee of '95 . . . . $150.00

EXPENSES.

Watchers $15.00
Campaign expenses 35.00
Prosecuting illegal voters 50.00
                                                  ——————   100.00

                    Balance . . . . $ 50.00

SUMMARY.

Club receipts raised by and from members $373.25
Receipts from Committee of '95 . . . .   150.00
                                                   —————— $523.25
Total expenses as above 422.80

                    Balance $100.45
Printing report 100.00

                    Balance . . . . $ 00.45

(58)

REPORT OF DIVISION WORK IN THE TWENTY-SECOND AND TWENTY-THIRD ELECTION DIVISIONS.

In pursuance of the request of the Civic Club, I present below my report of the recent canvass of the twenty-second and twenty-third divisions of the Seventh Ward, in the interest of Mrs. Sophia W. R. Williams and Mrs. Eliza B. Kirkbride, the candidates for school directors, nominated by the Municipal League and endorsed by the Democratic party, from the names sent in by the Civic Club.

These two divisions are particularly interesting because they are the only Democratic ones in the ward. On this account, as well as because of the thorough Municipal League work done there, they were easy to canvass. The twenty-third contains a large number of active Municipal League workers, and the twenty-second is in that intelligently receptive state which precedes conviction.

The twenty-third, bounded by the south side of Spruce Street, west side of Twenty-second Street, south side of Pine Street, and west by the Schuylkill, is my own division, and I helped Mrs. Isaac Starr, our chairman, to canvass it. We had a very interesting parlor meeting at my house, which was well attended, and where Mrs. Kirkbride, Mrs. Mumford, Mr. Wallerstein, and Mr. Eyre spoke.

This division contains a large proportion of people in the better classes of life, and many from the respectable working classes. On the other hand it harbors some very degraded specimens of humanity; among these being the descendants of the once notorious Schuylkill Rangers.*

* [In the period before the Consolidation Act of Philadelphia and for some time after, the edge of the city along the Schuylkill, then the limit of the old charter city, was the haunt of riotous and unruly gangs of ruffian marauders, old and

(59)

We laid our division out in parts, and each worker canvassed her share thoroughly. What may be called the "toughest" part luckily fell to Miss Esther Starr and me, and we found it much more exciting and interesting than the more respectable streets would have been.

In our canvassing on Kent Street, a narrow street running between Pine Street and DeLancey Place, Twenty-second Street and the river, we were warned against visiting one house. If the voter had "a glass in his head," as the neighbors expressed it, we might be roughly treated. We braved him, however, found him quite sober, and very intelligent, and we went joyfully on our way, upon his declaring he was "for the women every time," and would come to our next meeting. He did appear, but in such a state that he came very near being ejected. He interrupted the speakers continually, and embarrassed me *somewhat*, after the meeting, by grasping me by both hands and announcing to everyone that I was his "gal." Imagine how discouraged we felt about him, whom we had thought our shining light in Kent Street. Our trust, however, was not entirely misplaced, for to his everlasting credit be it said that he turned up sober on election day, voted for us himself, and brought several others to do likewise.

In contrast to our experiences in what are called the back streets, was the following: I went to call on one of my own friends, and was fortunate enough to encounter the "head of the house." He listened patiently to all I had to say, and then remarked: "I am proud to say I have not voted for twenty years, and I have made a vow never to vote again."

This from a man who should be a useful citizen. I was afraid I had wasted my time on him, but he did say in parting that he was tempted this year to vote for the women on the

young, known as "Schuylkill Rangers," who made both life and property unsafe and insecure by night and day. The boundaries of the old divisions of the present city to which the semi-criminal, lawless classes gravitated, because escape from the police was easy across the artificial civic boundary, still at most points retain traces of old conditions.—THE EDITOR.]

school boards. His wife declared that she only wished she had his chance to vote !

In canvassing the various classes of voters, we were much impressed by the marked contrast in the attitude of the richer, better, and more educated classes toward municipal politics, as distinguished from that of the so-called ignorant people in the small streets. On Spruce Street, Pine Street, DeLancey and Trinity Places, many voters asked the following questions :

"When *is* next election day?"
"What candidates, besides the Mayor, are to be voted for?"
"What is the number of this division?"
"How is this ward bounded anyhow?" etc.

While in the small streets the voter appeared to know all these facts quite as well as the canvassers.

In the small streets, in the midst of all the wretchedness, dirt and ignorance, there was scarcely a single instance of indifference to questions of government. In the large streets we found citizens whose bosoms swelled with pride, as they declared: "I never vote. It is hopeless to obtain good government." "A vote is a privilege, not a duty." "Free government and universal suffrage are humbugs, and, moreover, women had better not meddle in politics." One woman, an acquaintance of mine whom I asked to help me canvass the division in which she lived, replied that she did not "exactly approve of the Civic Club," and thought canvassing "unwomanly." The reflections that such a state of affairs arouses are most serious.

The vote for 1895 and 1894 in the twenty-third division for school directors was :

1895.		1894.	
Shedaker, R.	84	Durham, R.	76
Esray, R.	80	Hastings, R.	78
Howard, R.	82	Leiper, R.	78
Williams, C. C.	139	Pryor, Jr., D.	99
Kirkbride, C. C.	141		
Sellers, D.	132		

The twenty-second division is bounded by Pine Street, Twenty-second Street, South Street and Twenty-fourth Street. I was chairman, and Miss Starr, Miss Emily Smith, and Mrs. Bradbury Bedell were most efficient workers. This division contains very few of the richer and more refined people. It harbors three voters who have very much contaminated their immediate neighborhood, to which the peppermint test might be applied to purify its politics, *i. e.*, a school director who says '' the school board is not a fit place for women.'' It is needless to say that in none of these houses were we rapturously received, and we are *proud* that these men voted against the women school directors.

I sent for a man from Pine Street whom I have employed for years, explained our aim to him, and asked him to help us to elect our candidates to take care of his children in the schools. If he were not a solitary example I should think I had failed as a canvasser, for he replied, '' Mrs. Eyre, my vote cannot be bought.'' In Mrs. Starr's division somewhat the same thing happened to a fellow-worker who was told by a voter that his vote was worth one dollar, and his neighbor's two. These incidents show what a tremendous work lies before us, when even the voters who believe in us are on the lookout for the usual bribery. We had many complaints of the school in this division, and the heartrending tales of what the more delicate children suffer in recess in the school yard from the rough ones, are almost inconceivable.

This division is a very hopeful one, for the women in it are with us almost '' to a man,'' and the small minority of men against us we hope to convince before the next election. We have many friends here, and were it not for the immediate presence of the three men before mentioned, we should have had a much more glorious result.

The vote for 1895 and 1894 in the twenty-second division for school directors was:

1895		1894	
Shedaker, R.	112	Durham, R.	100
Esray, R.	107	Hastings, R.	100
Howard, R.	114	Leiper, R.	100
Williams, C. C.	132	Pryor, Jr., D.	118
Kirkbride, C. C.	131		
Sellers, D.	127		

The candidates, the secretaries of the Civic Club and of the Campaign Committee and I, went to every booth in the ward on election day, and were only invited to go through the booths of the twenty-second and twenty-third divisions. We thank the officials of these booths for a most interesting and novel sight.

The idea of women school directors is one that has come to stay, and I hope we all mean to continue in our work until we succeed. *We* are proud of *our* divisions, and we are encouraged to persevere until they are carried unanimously for good government. I, at least, have really enjoyed this campaign, and we have been brought into contact with life in a way that has helped to make more thoughtful women and more useful citizens of us all. The result all through this corrupt ward has been an encouragement to good government and the work of the Municipal League and Civic Club.

NINA B. EYRE.

2302 DeLancey Place.

THE COLLEGE SETTLEMENT'S SHARE IN THE RECENT CAMPAIGN.

The College Settlement always welcomes any opportunity to get better acquainted with its neighbors or to increase its accurate knowledge of the neighborhood. Therefore it gladly took advantage of the occasion offered by the Campaign Committee for the canvass of the first division of the Seventh Ward.

The Settlement is just outside this division, which is bounded by the south side of Lombard Street, the west side of Seventh Street, the north side of South Street and the east side of Ninth Street. It includes, therefore, both sides of Eighth Street from South to Lombard, Carver and Cullen Streets from Seventh to Eighth, McCann's, Turner's, Levy's, Brown's, Patton's and Yeager's Courts, Cedar Avenue, Cross Alley and Lombard Row.

According to the assessor's list the division has 255 voters, living in ninety-one houses. The voters are chiefly colored and men of foreign birth or parentage, and the party line almost coincides with the color line, the colored people being Republicans to a man, while the whites are, generally speaking, Democrats. The Republicans are in the majority, usually receiving about two-thirds of the votes cast in the division.

The work of the committee of the first division was done by five of the Settlement residents. A young man, one of the Settlement workers, made supplementary calls where it was thought a man might elicit facts which a woman could not. Every house in the division was visited twice and most of them three times. The caller was in every case courteously received and in all but a very few cases listened to with attention and apparent interest. In a few cases the courtesy was so pronounced, and the eagerness to give information

(64)

before it was asked for so marked, as to give rise to suspicions that there was something to conceal. In all such cases a visit paid by the gentleman assisted either in strengthening or confirming the suspicion.

The first visit paid to a house was to gather all the information possible. As many of the voters of this division are small shop-keepers living in the same house with their business it was possible to see a great many of the voters themselves. Remembering, however, the educational purposes of the campaign, an effort was made to see the woman of the house also and to interest her.

The caller did not hurry but took advantage of any opportunity offered for general conversation and in this way much was gained; for a little skillful guidance of the drift of the talk was often more effective than direct questioning. In this division it was generally safe to assume as a basis for work that knowing the color one knew the party, and the facts in the case usually developed in the course of the conversation. No promises were asked for, though many were volunteered.

In only a few cases were people found who decidedly opposed women on the school board, and those who opposed were as often women as men. Many of the men who were straight Republicans agreed that it was right and proper that women should be upon the board, and that it would probably result in the improvement of the school, but urged that inasmuch as they were upon the Democratic ticket they would feel bound to support that party in cases of a party vote in the board, and that therefore the Republican voter could not support them. Nothing could persuade some men that the women were not bound to vote with either party, but would give a conscience vote in all cases. The hold of the party upon the voter was everywhere apparent. In a few cases hints were thrown out, or even direct questions asked, as to the amount of money to be spent by the women in the campaign.

Questions were always asked as to the school children in the family, and any disposition to discuss the school or its management was encouraged with a view to finding out so far as possible the attitude of mind of the division toward the public schools. When the streets are swarming with little folks the small number of voters having children in school was quite surprising until the fact was recalled that the division is rapidly filling up with foreigners, whose children are in school, but who themselves are not yet naturalized. Lombard Street, too, has a considerable number of lodging houses patronized by unmarried men.

The criticisms upon the school and its management were seldom intelligent, and varied from the very general complaint of one old colored man who said that the school was so bad that his daughter " had removed herself of her own volition on account of almost complete nervous prostration," to that very specific charge of a white foreigner who said that her child's teacher being both deaf and blind could not see or hear when the pupils got into mischief and requested her removal! Some people seemed to think that if Mrs. Williams and Mrs. Kirkbride were elected it would be their duty to redress grievances of all sorts, and asked that such facts as that a man was out of work, or that a woman would not pay her child's board, be brought to their attention.

As there is a large percentage of residents in the neighborhood who are continually "on the move" it was not surprising that a large number of names should have been found on the assessor's list whose possessors no longer lived at the addresses given. About sixty names were found of those who had moved, were dead, did not exist, or were in prison. Of these over half belonged to the first class. Some houses used as political clubrooms or division headquarters undoubtedly were accredited with more voters than honestly belonged to them, but irregularities of this sort were almost impossible to prove.

The second visit was paid to give the invitation to the public meetings held in the Settlement Hall, and the third visit on the day before election was with the sample ballot which every one was delighted to get.

Two public meetings were held in the Settlement Hall. One on the afternoon of February 12 was addressed by Mrs. Williams, Mrs. Kirkbride, Mrs. Coppin, Mr. Salter, and Mr. Durham. There was a very small attendance, not over fifteen people outside of those specially interested being present. The second meeting on the evening before the election was better attended, though there were not as many at this as had been hoped. Before the meeting the Davis Cadets, a drill corps of forty boys who meet weekly at the Settlement, dressed in their uniforms and decorated with the "Women Want Women on the School Board" badges, marched through the streets of the first and second divisions. They were preceded by a drum and fife corps, and carried a large transparency, with the names of the candidates, the place of the meeting, etc., upon it. Although the little procession attracted a large crowd in the street, it did not succeed in filling the hall to overflowing. Still the meeting was a good one. The speakers were Mrs. Williams, Mrs. Kirkbride, Mrs. Coppin, Mr. Wallerstein and Dr. Morton.

In the canvass fifty-one votes were promised, and others seemed so favorably impressed that more were hoped for. But alas for hopes! The committee were doomed to disappointment. The returns of the first division showed only forty-five faithful to their promises. Mrs. Williams and Mrs. Kirkbride each receiving that number of votes. But the fact that they ran thirteen votes ahead of the man on the Democratic ticket was somewhat consoling. The Republican candidates polled 110, 105 and 105 votes respectively.

Late in the afternoon of election day a man prominent in division politics sent an urgent request to the chairman of the committee to call upon him at once. This she did not do. Possibly had she done so, and had the women's party not been the party of reform, something might have been done even at that late hour to have changed the results.

Of the judge and inspectors of election two were men notoriously unfit for their office. Had it seemed best to push the matter something might have been done to remove at least one of them. The third man was an intelligent, respectable and honest young man, and his presence and participation in the counting of the votes made it as certain as it can ever be in such cases that the ballots cast for the women in the first division were counted for them.

There are two chief reasons which the committee from the Settlement believe to be responsible for the meagerness of the direct results. First, the colored people are largely in the majority in this division. They are naturally strong Republicans and suspicious of anything Democratic. The women would undoubtedly have stood a better chance had their names appeared only on the ticket of the Municipal League. Secondly, it is much easier to vote the straight ticket by marking in the circle than to cross each separate name. This must be a great temptation to the illiterate and to the lazy. Were there a change in the methods used at present which should require all names to be marked the independent or reform candidate would stand a better chance.

Although disappointed in the material results, the educational effects of the canvass, the interest aroused in the candidacy of women, and the belief awakened that their presence on the school board will result in practical reforms in the public schools of the city, was seed sown which will bear fruit in the next campaign of the Civic Club.

KATHARINE BEMENT DAVIS,
Chairman.

The College Settlement,
617 St. Mary Street.

CALL OF MEETING FOR ORGANIZATION.

The following call was issued January 24, summoning a meeting of the members of the Civic Club in the Seventh Ward and other interested women, to form a ward organization:

SPECIAL MEETING OF THE JOINT COMMITTEE

OF THE

Departments of Education and Municipal Government of the Civic Club

ON

WOMEN ON SCHOOL BOARDS.

Your attendance is especially and particularly requested at the College of Physicians on Tuesday morning, January 29, at eleven o'clock, at a meeting to be held by the members of the Civic Club resident in the Seventh Ward, and others interested in the improvement of our schools, for the purpose of organizing a campaign committee to urge, by a personal canvass through the ward, a conscience vote for Mrs. S. W. R. Williams and Mrs. Eliza B. Kirkbride as school directors.

As the attendance at this meeting will be accepted as a gauge of the interest taken by you in this movement, your absence will be considered a serious loss to the cause.

Seventeen women from nine wards expressed themselves through the Civic Club as willing to serve on the school boards.

Their names were sent to the Democratic and Republican leaders and to the Municipal League. In the Seventh Ward the Municipal League nominated Mrs. Sophia W. R. Williams and Mrs. Eliza B. Kirkbride for school directors, and later they were endorsed by the Democratic party.

It has been proposed to appoint a committee, in each of the twenty-six divisions of the ward, to canvass carefully the ward and to secure the largest possible non-partisan vote for these women.

It is not intended to oppose any other candidates nor share the canvass of any political party.

The election of Mrs. Sophia W. R. Williams and Mrs. Eliza B. Kirkbride is asked solely because it is best for the schools of the section. But more important than their election is the beginning of the ward organization of women to work for the right, and to develop higher standards of municipal action.

MARY E. MUMFORD,
Chairman of Joint Committee.

EDITH WETHERILL,
Secretary of Joint Committee.

PLAN OF CAMPAIGN MADE BY THE EMERGENCY COMMITTEE

TO THE JOINT MEETING OF THE EDUCATIONAL AND MUNICI-
PAL DEPARTMENTS OF THE CLUB, AT THE COLLEGE
OF PHYSICIANS AND SURGEONS, ON TUES-
DAY MORNING, JANUARY 29, 1895.

Mrs. President and Ladies of the Committee:—In a general way, what is proposed is to reach every woman in the Seventh Ward by house to house visits, in which the women of the house will be *seen* and their assistance *asked* in the effort to poll a conscience vote for the two women who have been nominated candidates for school directors, not for any party, but in the interests of better schools.

The first thing which must be remembered is the boundary of the Seventh Ward, which extends from the west side of Seventh Street to the Schuylkill, and from the south side of Spruce Street to the north side of South Street.

From now on make it a point to ask every man you know living within these boundaries to vote for the two women for school directors, and ask every other woman to ask the same of every man she knows.

This ward at the next election chooses four school directors. The ticket presented to the voters will have on it three candidates named by the Republicans and three by the Municipal League and the Democrats. The three named by the Municipal League and the Democrats are two of them the women who were named by the Civic Club—Mrs. Kirkbride and myself. As the ward is a strong Republican ward, and we are seeking to make a non-partisan canvass, it is important that in asking for votes, Mrs. Kirkbride and myself should be spoken of as on the ticket of the Municipal League, rather than on the Democratic ticket, though

(71)

as a matter of fact we appear on both.   I have asked Mrs.
Kirkbride to speak of the arguments which are to be urged
in order to persuade women and particularly the mothers of
school children, to secure votes for your candidates.

It is my purpose in what follows to direct your attention
to the organization by which the work is to be done,
because except by organization, the strictest obedience and
the closest attention to detail, it would be idle for us to
expect to reach 6000 voters in three weeks.   As each woman,
however, who is asked to join in this work, has only to visit
thirty or forty houses in the next ten days, and make a five
to ten minutes' visit in each, there is no reason why we
should not be successful, at least, in letting every voter know
through some woman that he ought to vote for the two
women in order to secure better schools.

The Seventh Ward is divided into twenty-six election
districts.   The boundaries are on the map of the ward,
which I hold, and I hope each woman here will, after this
meeting, look at the map and fix in her mind the boundaries
of the division in which she lives or to which she is assigned.
These divisions average about 250 voters who live in about
200 houses.   In each division there has been appointed a
chairman from the Civic Club, and with her two members
of the club are associated, residing in the division, as far
as possible, but always in the ward.   These three constitute
the division committee, and to them are to be added other
women to work on the committees, and to come to the meetings of the "general committee," composed of all the
division committee women from the ward and from outside
the ward, who are as much interested in securing good
schools as any member of the Civic Club.

The Civic Club has appointed a campaign committee,
consisting of Mrs. J. Lewis Parks, Mrs. N. Dubois Miller,
Mrs. Kirkbride and myself, with Miss Edith Wetherill, the
secretary of the Municipal Department, as secretary.   The
Civic Club holds this committee responsible for the ward,

and this committee holds each chairman responsible for *her* division, and each chairman must divide up her division between the members of her committee, keeping a portion for herself and holding each member responsible for her share.

If the work is properly done at the end of about ten days from now, when the chairmen are called together, each will be able to make a report, something like this: "In my division there are 258 voters and 237 houses. Of these houses 210 have been visited and the women seen, and asked to work to secure a vote for the two women. In ten houses we have been unable to see the women, and in five have been refused admittance. In regard to 110 voters, we have received assurances that they will vote for the women candidates, twenty voters are doubtful, 103 will vote the regular Republican ticket, and there are twenty-five voters in regard to which no information was obtained." This would be a model report. I don't think this will be possible in many divisions, but ten days from now it ought to be possible to report that every house has been visited and each chairman ought to be able to make an approximate report as to the canvass. At present your division is practically unknown to you.

It has always seemed to me one of the sad things in city life that we are willing to live without coming in civic contact with those closest around us, and without trying to help and to direct them to get better things in government and in streets and in schools. For myself, I will be satisfied if the only result of this campaign were to make us all acquainted with the divisions in which we live, and lay the foundations of a neighborhood feeling in this ward.

Each chairman will be given two lists of the voters in her division. One of them will be pasted in a little book, with a blank opposite each name, and in this blank she must enter the information gained, particularly the women who influence this vote as wife, sister or mother, whether children are sent from the house to the public schools, and the way the man

usually votes and will vote this time on school directors.
This record must be carefully kept and returned to the committee at the close of the campaign, as it will be an invaluable
record for our effort to poll a conscience vote at the next
election. The other list of voters furnished to each chairman ought to be cut up and divided among the women on
the committee of that division, for use in their canvass.

It will be necessary for each chairman to call together
her committee at once and go over the list of voters together,
checking off the information any member of the committee
may already have in regard to any voter. The assessor's
list of voters gives the occupation and address of each voter,
also states whether they are boarders or householders.

In this house to house canvass we must not hesitate to go
to the big houses because the vote in those houses will generally be in our favor, when our object is explained, but is
cast by men who half the time will not take the trouble to
vote. We must not hesitate to go to the small houses,
because this is the vote which we need to gain.

In a large number of cases the blue book will give the
names of the women in the house and it will be well to enter
this opposite the names in the voters' lists.

Mrs. Kirkbride has explained the general argument and
Mrs. Mumford the special needs of the schools. I leave it
to your own tact how this is to be presented to the women
you see. The important thing is to make it perfectly clear
that you are asking a vote for Mrs. Eliza B. Kirkbride and
Mrs. Sophia W. R. Williams for school directors. Later you
will take or send to each woman whom you have seen, a
specimen ballot and ask her to get her voter to check his
vote like that. For this purpose it is important to know how
the voter usually votes, if you can find this out without
prying.

After this house to house work has been done for a few
days, and it must begin at once for we have no time to lose,
we will begin holding school director teas or parlor meetings,

division by division, at which the women whom you have seen will be brought together and addressed by Mrs. Kirkbride and other winning speakers. It will be the duty of each chairman to begin at once, preparing for these school director teas which will simply be meetings under another name, and can be held in private houses, church chapels or halls as seems best in each division.

The Campaign Committee will call together from time to time the chairmen of the divisions and this general committee of all the women engaged in the work, will be called together two weeks from to-day to hear reports from the divisions. Let me in closing ask all the chairmen to remain after this meeting to receive their division lists and special instructions.

The Campaign Committee will meet every day at half past ten o'clock at Mrs. Kirkbride's, 1406 Spruce street, and will be glad to see there every chairman of committees and other division workers, in order to give information and instruction.

SOPHIA WELLS ROYCE WILLIAMS.

INSTRUCTIONS TO CHAIRMEN OF DIVISION CAMPAIGN COMMITTEES.

The Special Campaign Committee meets daily at 1406 Spruce street, at 10.30 a. m., to meet chairmen of division committees and their workers.

Circulars and other literature for distribution may be found at 1406 Spruce street.

SUGGESTIONS TO CHAIRMEN.

Call your committees together at once ; also your outside workers.

Define clearly to all your workers the boundaries of your division.

Go over the assessor's list of your division with your workers, and note carefully any items of personal knowledge likely to be useful in the campaign.

Divide the houses to be visited among the workers, and hold each responsible for her share.

Two workers can probably best visit together.

USE OF THE DIVISION BOOK.

1. Note the name of the woman most likely to influence a vote, and her relationship to the voter.

2. Note each family with children at the public schools.

3. Note the ticket usually voted by each man.

Take special care of the books and return to 1406 Spruce street, at the end of the campaign.

MODEL REPORT AFTER TEN DAYS' WORK.

In my division, the ———, there are 258 voters and 237 houses ; 210 houses visited, women seen and asked to secure votes ; at ten houses unable to see women, or admittance refused. From 110 voters assurances received of votes for women school directors ; 20 voters doubtful ; 103 will vote regular Republican ticket ; of 25 voters, no information.

CIVIC CLUB.

1. Remember, your first object is to persuade the women whom you see to influence a voter to mark with a cross the names of Mrs. Sophia W. R. Williams and Mrs. Eliza B. Kirkbride, or if you can, instead, see the voter directly, so much the better.

2. Be sure that whoever you talk to understands distinctly that you are asking for votes for the two women nominated for school directors in the Seventh Ward, whose names will appear on the ticket under the heading "Municipal League" or "Democratic."

3. In the course of the conversation be sure to ask the number of the house, and whether the person or persons entered in your assessor's list as living there live in the house or live somewhere else, and if so, where they live, if known. Also, whether they vote the Democratic or Republican ticket. If Democratic, your task is easy, as they will vote for the ticket anyway, but be sure to ask them to be *certain to vote for the two women* and *not* to strike out their names. The reason why you want to find out whether a voter is Democratic or Republican is because a different specimen ballot will have to be sent to the Republican from that sent to the Democratic voter.

4. Find also at each house if there are any children attending the public schools, and ask if the mothers have any suggestions to make for improvement in the treatment of the children, or complaint as to present treatment, as the two women, if elected, intended to be guided by the opinions of the mothers of the ward in these matters.

5. Make prompt and careful notes of all you learn of each name each time, and not once trust to memory, as these records will be most important for the future use of the Civic Club.

6. In case any voter is not living at the number given in the list furnished you, ask if he is living at the adjoining house, and if not, make a separate list of all such names, which are, of course, fraudulent. Mark plainly with the ward divisions, sign your name to it, and send at once to to the chairman of your division.

7. Again, remember, your first object is to persuade the women whom you see to influence a voter to mark with a cross the names of Mrs. Sophia W. R. Williams and Mrs. Eliza B. Kirkbride, or if you can, instead, see the voter directly, so much the better.

(77)

ADDRESS TO THE WOMEN OF THE WARD,

"NEIGHBORS AND FRIENDS."

The following address to the women of the Seventh Ward was circulated broad-cast through the ward, and left at every house, as well as printed on a one sheet poster and billed through the ward two days before election.

CIVIC CLUB.

To Our Neighbors and Friends, the Women of the Seventh Ward:

We feel sure of your sympathy when we appeal to you to do all that you can to secure the election to your school board of two women who have been nominated to that office in the Seventh Section. Every school board should have women upon it for these reasons :

First. They represent the mothers, who know best how to deal with the needs of children.

Second. They can understand and assist the teachers, nearly all of whom are women.

Third. They will, as far as they possibly can, remove the schools from the influence of politics.

Fourth. They have no ambitions to serve, but offer themselves for the simple good of the children and the community.

The Civic Club looks confidently to you to help in this matter.

Ask voters to vote for better schools in the ward by making a cross against the name of each of the two women for school directors, SOPHIA W. R. WILLIAMS and ELIZA B. KIRKBRIDE.

MID-CANVASS REPORT MADE BY THE EMERGENCY COMMITTEE

TO THE JOINT MEETING OF THE EDUCATIONAL AND MUNI-
CIPAL DEPARTMENTS OF THE CIVIC CLUB, AT THE
COLLEGE OF PHYSICIANS AND SURGEONS, ON
TUESDAY MORNING, FEBRUARY 12, 1895.

The object of the work, which has been thus far done, has been the persuasion of voters, information as to the character of the vote, and self-education as to the workers.

Whatever else has been done, whatever has succeeded or failed, I feel certain the workers themselves have gotten much self-education out of it all.

The machine makes every effort in the last week to clinch the work already done, and so successfully does it do this, that the night before an election of any importance, out of 130,000 votes in the whole city, they will be able to predict with absolute certainty 129,000 of these votes. Keeping this in mind, if we would succeed, there is still much work to be done, particularly in the distribution of specimen ballots, in using the notes, in writing letters, seeing doubtful people, seeing the women who have promised to induce their husbands to vote and finding out if they have succeeded.

Lastly, this work is not done for this election. It has been done to produce a permanent personal influence for good in the ward. Each of the chairmen who lives in the division where she has worked and the others, as far as possible, ought to do everything they can in this last week, to establish personal relations, in order to make it natural and easy one year from now, to do the same work over again, to make this effort for some other candidate who will be more successful than I fear Mrs. Kirkbride and I can expect to be, beginning in a ward with 4000 majority against us and with no organization.

During the last week I have been brought in contact with a good many politicians, who all say that with persistent effort of this kind we could take the schools out of politics in from three to five years.

I want to say one thing more, too much care cannot be exercised by the visitors in using names, no name on the ticket beyond that of the two women candidates must be referred to or talked about in their visits. We hear Mr. Shedaker has been very much offended by hearing that one of the visitors said he could not read or write. This, of course, was a mistake, as we all know that he is a most excellent member of the school board of the Seventh Ward, but this shows the necessity of care.

The badges which the chairmen will receive at the end of this meeting, were kindly presented by Mrs. Willis K. Martin, to whom our thanks are due. We hope the chairman will be able to induce a great many women to wear them until after the election.

Will the chairmen please remain after the meeting to receive ballots, maps and badges for distribution in their several divisions.

SOPHIA WELLS ROYCE WILLIAMS.

APPENDIX.

In addition to the "posters" and "flies" already noted, containing the Civic Club address to the women of the ward, the following documents were issued :

About 10,000 copies of the following extract from the Philadelphia *Press* were circulated:

UNHEALTHY SCHOOLHOUSES.

The Philadelphia city government has a good many reports which are depressing reading to the lover of his kind, but we doubt if there is any one of them more depressing than a file of the reports of Dr. J. Howard Taylor, medical inspector to the Board of Health, of which the last was made last week.

Taking these reports for ten years back, and both the condition of the schools and the time it takes to cure their evils become plain. From three to five years are needed to mend a leaking latrine in a schoolhouse which in a private dwelling would be attended to in a week. For seven years, since 1888, in the Seventh Ward, at Nineteenth and Addison, the defective grade in the boys' yard has been reported upon. Seven times the sectional board has been told yearly that after a rain the water stands in this yard several inches deep, and in 1895 the defect remains as in 1887.

The reports which Dr. Taylor has made have had some effect, and the reforms he urges ought to be adopted. By ten years of effort the water closets have nearly all been changed. Now the ventilation needs to be improved. Children slightly ill ought to be promptly examined to learn if they have contagious diseases. The prescribed term of exclusion after a pupil has had any such illness ought to be rigidly enforced. Children ought not to be sent to inquire after their absent playmates. The children's wraps and winter garments ought not to be hung up in closets together, making infection easy.

These reforms are easy and cheap, but they involve a sedulous supervision of the schools which men on the sectional school boards never have given and never will. Dr. Taylor's reports constitute the strongest possible argument for the election of the women nominated for school directors in the Seventh, Fifteenth and Twenty-fourth Wards. The Civic Club ought to continue its efforts to place women on the sectional school boards until they are present on them in every ward in the city.

———————

Ask voters to vote for better schools in the Seventh Ward by making a cross against the name of each of the two women for School Directors,

SOPHIA W. R. WILLIAMS
and ELIZA B. KIRKBRIDE.

(81)

APPEAL TO VOTERS.

On the eve of election the following appeal was printed on a slip of heavy paper with broad margins, on which a personal note could be written and 500 copies were sent, accompanied by a personal appeal to acquaintances and friends in the ward :

Be sure to vote on Tuesday, February 19, and when you vote, under school directors, cross the names of

SOPHIA W. R. WILLIAMS

AND

ELIZA B. KIRKBRIDE,

who are under the Municipal League and Democratic caption in the Seventh Ward.

INSTRUCTIONS TO ELECTION OFFICERS.

The "Baker Ballot Law" in Pennsylvania (Act of June 10, 1893), permits voters to mark with a cross the circle opposite the party name, thus voting for all the candidates of the party or by marking with a cross opposite the name of each candidate individually to vote for each separately. This raised the possibility that Republican voters would mark the circle opposite the name of their party and place a cross opposite the names of the women candidates, raising a question as to which cross decided their vote. In view of this contingency this statement of law was sent to every election officer in the ward, summarizing the judicial interpretation of the twenty-seventh section of the Act.

SEVENTH WARD

Woman's Campaign Committee,

Civic Club.

PHILADELPHIA, February 18, 1895.

The following statement of law is sent to every election officer in the Seventh Ward upon the advice of counsel :—

HOW TO COUNT THE VOTE.

Judge Finletter in Philadelphia, Judge Schuyler in Northampton County and Judge Sittser in Sullivan County, have decided, that where a vote is cast for all the names in a party column by making a cross at the head of the column, and in addition the voter makes a cross opposite the name of a candidate for one of the same offices, in another column, **this latter vote is to be counted,** and not the name for the same office in party column.

Therefore, if a voter marks the individual names of Mrs. Williams and Mrs. Kirkbride for school directors in **any** column, the votes thus cast for them **must be counted,** and not the names of other candidates for the same office in the column which has a cross at the top.

An election officer who does not heed this notice cannot claim that he is ignorant of the law.

M. C. WISTER,
Chairman Woman's Campaign Committee.

(83)

CAMPAIGN BADGE.

The following was printed in red on ribbon and 500 worn in work in the ward. A like caption was placed on a banner displayed election day at every polling place.

WOMEN WANT

WOMEN

ON

SCHOOL BOARDS

TO CARE FOR

THEIR CHILDREN.

CIVIC CLUB.

First Division.

Miss KATHARINE B. DAVIS, *Chairman*,
College Settlement.
Miss MARY B. LIPPINCOTT,
College Settlement.
Miss FRANCES M. TYLER,
College Settlement.

Miss MARY B. HEATH,
College Settlement.
Miss EMMA I. BETTES,
College Settlement.
Mr. LUCIAN BERRY,
Seventh and Carver Streets.

Second Division.

Mrs. J. LEWIS PARKS, *Chairman*,
717 Pine Street.

Mrs. CHARLES W. NOLEN,
714 Pine Street.

Miss ELIZABETH MORRIS,
718 Pine Street.

Third Division.

Mrs. WILLIAM KRAUSE, *Chairman*,
903 Clinton Street.
Miss ANNA J. MORRIS,
318 South Tenth Street.

Mrs. PANZERBIELER,
708 Washington Square.
Miss LOUISE BETTS EDWARDS,
625 Spruce Street.

Fourth Division.

Mrs. J. NORMAN JACKSON, *Chairman*,
1009 Pine Street.

Mrs. EDWARD R. FELL,
1030 Spruce Street.

Mrs. T. MORRIS KNIGHT,
1030 Spruce Street.

Fifth Division.

The visiting was done by a paid worker.

Sixth Division.

Mrs. CLIFFORD LEWIS, *Chairman*,
313 South Twelfth Street.
Mrs. HOWARD WOOD,
1016 Spruce Street.
Miss HELEN B. WOOD,
1016 Spruce Street.
Miss ALICE PRIME,
1008 Spruce Street.

Miss CHARLOTTE W. HARE,
1013 Clinton Street.
Miss MARY H. WILSON,
1106 Spruce Street.
Miss JULIA WINSLOW DICKERSON,
"The Gladstone."
Miss M. de BENNEVILLE,
1716 Pine Street.

Seventh Division.

Mrs. RICHARD STOCKTON HUNTER,
  Chairman, 1413 Locust Street.
Mrs. SAMUEL LOWRIE,
  1827 Pine Street.
Mrs. J. CHESTON MORRIS,
  1514 Spruce Street.
Mrs. SAMUEL DICKSON,
  901 Clinton Street.

Miss MARIE LANSDALE,
  921 Clinton Street.
Miss ALICE CUSHMAN,
  1340 Walnut Street.
Mrs. WALTER COPE,
  Chestnut Hill.
Miss MARIA BLANCHARD,
  1511 Walnut Street.

Eighth Division.

Mrs. N. DUBOIS MILLER, *Chairman*,
  1230 Spruce Street.
Mrs. LAURA SYLVESTER,
  39 South Nineteenth Street.

Mrs. CHANCELLOR C. ENGLISH,
  1527 Spruce Street.
Miss EDITH WETHERILL,
  Chalkley Hall.

Mrs. WM. M. SALTER,
  1415 Walnut Street.

Ninth Division.

Miss PHEBE A. HOUGH, *Chairman*,
  1340 Spruce Street.
Miss MARY C. COXE,
  1302 Pine Street.

Mrs. DAVID LIGHTNER WITMER,
  1314 Spruce Street.
Mrs. JOHN VAN KIRK,
  1333 Pine Street.

Miss ELIZABETH W. MOSELEY,
  1333 Pine Street.

Tenth Division.

MISS MARY C. COXE, *Chairman*,
  1302 Pine Street.

Miss BEULAH H. JENKS,
  2004 Arch Street.

Miss ANNA F. RANDOLPH,
  2002 Arch Street.

Eleventh Division.

Mrs. EDWARD WETHERILL, *Chairman*,
  Chalkley Hall.

Miss EDITH HOWARD COOKE,
  1700 Pine Street.

Madame E. NICHOLAI,
  331 South Broad Street.

Twelfth Division.

This division had no chairman. The work was done by:

Mrs. GEORGE REXAMER,
  329 South Sixteenth Street.
Miss ELIZABETH LEIGHTON LEE,
  1532 Pine Street.

Miss LOUISE BETTS EDWARDS,
  625 Spruce Street.
Miss ELIZABETH S. LOWRY,
  422 South Broad Street.

Thirteenth Division.

Mrs. NATHAN F. MOSSELLE, *Chairman*,
  1432 Lombard Street.
Miss JULIA F. JONES,
  1524 Lombard Street.

Miss ETTIE CLEMENS,
  620 South Broad Street.
Mrs. ELLA McGRUDER,
  512 South Fifteenth Street.

Miss ANNA JONES,
  1524 Lombard Street.

www.ingramcontent.com/pod-product-compliance
Lightning Source LLC
Chambersburg PA
CBHW031445270326
41930CB00007B/881